SALVATION
A Journey from Death to Life

SALVATION

A Journey from Death to Life

C. L. Stubblefield, Sr., PhD

ISBN: 978-1-7322004-0-1

TABLE OF CONTENTS

DEDICATION

I dedicate this book to my sons, Cedrick Jr., Kyle, and Sean, and the legacy they represent. Although written for an audience of three, this book is purposed to bridge the gap of time, affording me the opportunity to me speak from an eventual grave and connect with generations to come. My grandfather, Pastor Isaac Stubblefield, gave my father what I now give to you: the wisdom of God's word. Pass it on.

ACKNOWLEDGEMENTS

Thanks to God who gives us the victory. There are so many people who contributed directly and indirectly to the completion of this book. Thanks to the pastors who taught and mentored me in God's word. Thanks to the ministers who sharpened me throughout the years by challenging my thoughts, beliefs, and stances. Thanks to family and friends who lent me their unwavering support and encouragement. As it pertains to my motivation to publishing this book, there are some who I must mention by name.

First, thank you Arnold and Ruby Stubblefield. You have been my biggest fans. Like the parent who runs alongside a child learning to ride a bicycle for the first time, you pushed me as fast as you could in every facet of my development and released me with the task of remaining upright. As I rode and still ride the bike of life, I can still hear you behind me, cheering me on. "You can do it Cedrick! Keep it up...DON'T STOP PEDALING!" You endowed me with the momentum needed to keep me upright in uncertain times.

Secondly, thank you Cedric Lang. This book is the product of our friendship. When you recruited me to write the foreword for your book, *The Time is Now,* you set the course for this book. Furthermore, your persistence in encouraging me to publish my thoughts motivated me to finish it. Thank you for your inspiration.

Finally, thank you Tamico, Cedrick Jr., Kyle, and Sean. Tamico, you are my rock, the wife I don't deserve. Cedrick, Kyle, and Sean, you are my life's work. This book is dedicated to and written for you. Your mother and I are as committed to your well-being as we were the day you entered our lives and are proud of your ability to stay upright on a path that has been filled with obstacles.

PREFACE

Stephen R. Covey, author of *First Things First*, introduced a persuasive illustration, demonstrating the importance of prioritizing and focusing on the principal things of life. Using a mason jar, rocks, and gravel, he postulated that the order in which we accomplish tasks can be critical. First, he poured gravel into the jar and placed the rocks on top. They would not all fit. The opposite occurred when he filled the jar with the "big rocks" prior to adding the gravel. His point? If you prioritize the "big rocks" first, the other things will all fall into place (Covey, Stephen A, et. al. 1994).

This book focuses on the "big rocks" of salvation. Christians tend to get sidetracked by the "little rocks" of the faith. We are often preoccupied with what clothes are appropriate, what hair styles are acceptable, how much makeup is too much, how many church members do we have, how much money do we raise, who do we know, who knows our name, and the list goes on. I won't debate the merits of such things, but I am confident they are not among the core aspects of salvation.

We spend a significant amount of time assimilating new believers into our Christian culture by pouring into them countless "little rocks." Ultimately, they rarely learn the most important aspects of our faith. The goal of this book is to focus our attention to the "big rocks" and discuss them in the context of God's plan for human restoration.

Each chapter provides an independent study of the critical aspects of salvation. This study guide will test the accuracy of the reader's beliefs, preconceptions, and doctrines. We will explore the fall of man, God's covenant and relationship with mankind, and many other "big rocks" necessary to understand God's holistic plan of salvation. The reader will ultimately see their destiny through the lens of God's perfect plan.

Casual reader beware. This book is for those who value their relationship with God and are committed to understanding what they claim to believe. Therefore, the entertainment value of this book is low. Those seeking self-help messages will likewise not find satisfaction. However, those who desire to help themselves to the word of God and seek to confidently explain their faith will cherish every moment spent within the pages that follow. If you can relate to the latter, you have the book, now get your Bible, and let's begin.

INTRODUCTION

When I began writing this book, my sole objective was to simply compile revelations gleamed from scripture as they pertained to soteriology, the doctrine of salvation. As I transcribed my thoughts, God began to illuminate His word, and I realized that the things revealed were but a glimpse of what He intended to impart. Soon, I discovered the simplicity of salvation as well as its complexity.

Most things in life appear simple, but unseen complexities lurk beneath the surface. Computers, for instance, are perfect examples of simplicity disguising complexity. Those who design computers aim to make them as user-friendly as possible. Companies that achieve the most modern, practical, convenient, and applicable design should expect to sell the most computers – if we ignore the power of marketing. The number of American households owning at least one computer increased from 8.2% to 75.6% from 1984 to 2011 (U.S. Census Bureau 2013). Therefore, we can assume that among those that are well acquainted with their computers can at least surf the web, draft a document, check email, track friends on Facebook, etc. However, most lack the knowledge necessary to appreciate the complex code and circuitry required to perform these actions.

If you have worked with computers, you know that turning them on is simple, opening a file is simple, sending an e-mail is simple, and turning them off is simple. It's what we find on the inside of the computer that makes it a complex machine. There are wires, gadgets, drives, motherboards, fuses, capacitors, processors, etc., which are quite confusing to the unfamiliar eye. Likewise, when you unscrew the panel of salvation and look inside, you will see things that are not understandable without being led by the One who provided the inspiration and dictation of its contents. God made salvation simple for us to obtain, but His plan to make it a reality is complex and strewn with manifold mysteries.

God purchased salvation and offers it to everyone as a free gift with no strings attached. This is the simplicity of the gospel or "good news." The familiar verse in the book of John says it best: "For

God so loved the world that He gave his only begotten Son, that whosoever believeth in Him should not perish, but have everlasting life" (John 3:16). It could not be simpler. Deny Him as truth and perish, or accept Him as truth and live eternally.

The intent of this book is to help potential believers make the right choice, provide new converts with a basic understanding of salvation, and stimulate spiritual growth and understanding in mature believers. In the chapters that follow, we will go behind the panel and expose the inner workings of salvation. We will explore, define, and seek to understand the greatest miracle God has ever performed, the simple but complex work of salvation.

There are so many aspects of salvation; no one could compile or explain them all in a single, comprehensive document. The Bible, in its completeness, does not explicitly explain all the mysteries of salvation. It would take countless years to completely articulate the doctrine of salvation.

Mysteries are revealed as we pray and study God's word, but in all my praying and studying, I've discovered that there is so much more to God than I can imagine. The more I know, the more I realize how much I don't know. God reveals truths to me, others, and to you. Therefore, we must view what God reveals to us, in light of what He reveals to others. In this way, Christian fellowship presents the opportunity for believer's to enrich their spiritual understanding through joint knowledge.

Chapter 1

BROKEN RELATIONSHIP

So God created man in his own image, in the
image of God created he him; male and female
created he them.
Genesis 1:27

Those who trust in God must find the strength
and faith to reconcile historical facts, scientific
theories, and philosophical rationalizations that
appear to stand in opposition to the biblical account
of the human existence. For example, archeologists
have discovered fossils of creatures never mentioned
from Genesis to Revelation. In fact, there are
hundreds of dinosaur parks and museums across the
country and the world. How can creatures so
massive be left out of the book designed to teach man
his history and lead him to his God? Surely an
omniscient God would have known that man would
unearth the bones of these creatures.

Many have suffered turmoil, grief, and strife at the hands of humanity and natural disasters. Countless people lost their lives in World War I and II, American Civil War, Vietnam War, Gulf War I and II, and several in between. The African slave trade, Christian crusades, and genocide of Jews at the hands of Nazi Germany were massacres committed without an appreciable respect for life. The devastation and loss of life resulting from humanity's violent tendencies is only rivaled by earthquakes, tsunamis, tornados, wildfires, hurricanes, and winter storms, leaving us without a suitable defense for their fury. How could He allow this to be? Surely an omnipotent God could prevent such atrocities.

Others say that history is written by the victor and suggest that the idea of an unadulterated biblical history is a naive notion. Why would He allow such men of bad character to annotate and translate His ideas for future generations? A God of perfection would not allow his virtue to be tainted by evil men. In their search for God, for some, these are stumbling blocks in the path to spiritual liberty.

I don't claim to have all the answers to these difficult questions, but most can be answered in

Genesis 1:1. The first four words of the Bible are "In the beginning God..." Every word thereafter is written that man may know and understand his purpose and God's will. We often assume that the beginning is a reference to the beginning of time. Well, it is and it isn't. This "beginning" is a reference to the time of man's existence. He began creation with the heavens and the earth. Scientists say it took millions of years for the earth/universe to transition from a state of chaos to a state predictable and hospitable enough to sustain life. However, God said He took a planet that "was without form and void" and shaped it in one day. I do not have a problem believing both.

The two views are easily reconciled when we follow the framework of Newton's first law of motion (Holton 1992). From the motion of the stars, we discover that the earth spins, but the rotation is not apparent to those who are rotating with the earth. We also know that the sun rises and sets because the earth is spinning. Furthermore, man's concept of time is based on the sun rising and setting and how long it takes to complete the cycle. Prior to the rotation of the earth or its orbit around the sun, time for humanity was undefined. How would one define time in the absence of these markers?

This is not a hypothetical question. It is a great unknown. God created the earth on the first day, but the sun was not created until the fourth day. Prior to the existence of the sun and the moon, what constituted a day? How many hours were in the first day, which Genesis 1:5 calls the evening and morning? Is this a case where He made something in an instant with the semblance of time? Can it be compared to the miracle Jesus performed at a wedding feast in Cana, where He turned water into wine, which was better than the naturally aged wine provided earlier in the feast (John 2:1-10)? An all-powerful God could have made the heavens and the earth in an instant, but how long is an instant in the context of eternity? What is the conversion factor for the number of days it took to create the world without the sun verses with the sun as a reference?

After creating the earth and all that dwell therein, God made man. Adam was not made for companionship, as some suggest. He was made to maintain the earth and its inhabitants. This is not to say that God did not love his creation: He did. God was not lonely nor did He need someone to talk to. He made man to tend to His creation (Genesis 2:15).

God is a lover of life, and from Him, all life flows. Artists can only paint what they see; musicians can only play what they hear; writers can only inscribe what they feel; and only God can produce life. He is the reservoir of life. God spoke and life came forth, and He said it was good. On the sixth day, He made man after His own image and likeness. Now, when He looked at the earth, He saw somewhat of a reflection of Himself. This made the whole of creation, in His words, "very good."

The creation story, however, did not end with the making of man. The climax of the creation story happened when God made woman. She was the solution to man's innate need for companionship (Genesis 2:18). This gift of companionship was intended to be so strong that the man would forsake all earthly ties to become one with his wife. The resultant sense of devotion shared by Adam and Eve would ultimately take them on a life changing journey.

MISERY LOVES COMPANY

Consider The Source

> And the serpent said unto the woman, Ye shall
> not surely die.
> Genesis 3:4

The ability to discern between a true friend and those who simply present themselves as friends is an essential life skill. A friend's integrity is never lacking, and they will always have your best interest in mind. Eve failed to learn this valuable lesson. Not knowing that Jehovah is the greatest friend of all, she chose poorly from whom to take advice. Genesis 3:4 tells us that the serpent, whether a serpent possessed by Satan or Satan himself, was responsible for deceiving Eve and subsequently the fall of man.

The wise use the wisdom of others, but understanding the difference between wisdom and waste is critical. Wisdom, the ability to correctly apply knowledge, will afford you success. Waste, or that which is barren, will unnecessarily expend time and resource and put you on a fast train to failure.

Eve's decision should have been clear. If God created the serpent, how could the serpent be the wiser of the two? She should have considered the source and realized that listening to the serpent was a waste of time and energy, which would lead to a waste of resources. God, on the other hand, cannot lie. If He has sworn it, He will perform it (Psalms 119:106).

> And these words, which I command thee this day…thou shalt bind them for a sign upon thine hand, and they shall be as frontlets between thine eyes. And thou shalt write them upon the posts of thy house, and on thy gates. Deuteronomy 6:6-9

God's direction was clear, "the fruit of the tree which is in the midst of the garden…ye shall not eat." He did not mince words. In fact, He placed the tree in the middle of the garden – He did so knowing man would sin. Why didn't He put it in some obscure place? Maybe it would have been better for man if the tree was in some far corner; but doing so would have been highly uncharacteristic. When God speaks, He wants us to remember every word.

The highest form of flattery is imitation. Echoing someone's words is a clear indication that you were listening attentively. Furthermore, it is a sign that you were influenced by the words enough to remember them. God does not need nor seek our flattery, but He expects us to obey His instructions, which is incumbent upon remembering them.

The tree in the midst of the garden was a constant, physical reminder to Adam and Eve. It provided a visual stimulus to help them recall God's verbal command. We find a similar approach used in Numbers 15: 37-38. God instructed the Israelites to place blue tassels on the corner of their garments to remind them of His commands. In the case of Adam and Eve, the daily reminder did not work.

Unfortunately for Eve, the encounters with the tree of knowledge eventually introduced her to a temptation beyond her ability to resist. Remember, the tree was not meant to be a temptation but perhaps a reminder. God does not tempt man with evil (James 1:13). Were Adam and Eve tempted? Yes. The tree, therefore, transitioned from a reminder to a temptation when Eve entertained the idea of eating its fruit.

The Temptation

> But every man is tempted, when he is drawn
> away of his own lust, and enticed. Then when
> lust hath conceived, it bringeth forth sin: and
> sin, when it is finished, bringeth forth death.
> James 1:14-15

Sin begins with the consideration of an action contrary to God's will. Prior to Satan's temptation, eating the fruit was not an option. Satan's proposal made Eve curious. She must have thought, "Maybe I misunderstood God. Maybe I didn't get the story right. This tree looks like it is 'good for food.' Look! The fruit is so brilliant and 'pleasing to the eyes.' If it can 'make one wise,' why can't I be wise?"

The seed of sin was mentally planted by Satan, and Eve's imagination, fueled by desire, entertained the notion that fertilized the seed and brought about the conception of sin. The birth of sin followed. Eve's desire for preservation, pleasure, and power led to the entrance of sin into the world, and they remain to perpetuate its existence. John, in his first epistle, defines them as the "lust of the flesh, and the lust of the eyes, and the pride of life" (1 John 2:16).

Every sin is rooted in lust and pride. Eve first noted that the fruit was good for nourishment, which is required for preservation. There is no mistaking the fact that the body has cravings. Those of us who are dieting are intimately familiar with this temptation. Certain foods were never a "must have" until they became the foods we "can't have." However, everyone has the capacity to sustain their will power and resist the urge to give in to temptation.

Cheating happens when we entertain the idea that a little bit won't hurt. We elect to appease the flesh, but it never stops with a little bit. The flesh requires all or nothing. It will take a little for now anticipating that more will follow. Eve should have dismissed the notion of eating the fruit with the first temptation, the lust of the flesh.

By rationalizing the first temptation, Eve opened herself to more. As if the lust, desires, or drives of the flesh were not enough, now she had to contend with the lust of the eyes. She now faced the fact that the fruit appeared pleasing to the eyes (e.g. juicy, brilliant in color). The eye is one of our biggest offenders. This is the reference point from which images are created. Did Eve just look at the fruit or did she wonder how it tasted? Was it hard? Was it soft? Was it sweet? Was it sour?

Naturally, Eve, as she looked at the fruit, must have envisioned herself eating it. Looking, however, was not the sin. The sin was looking to lust (to please one's self). Jesus said that if a man looks on a woman to lust after her then he has sinned in his heart (Matthew 5:28). Perhaps Eve saw the fruit every day, but this was different. Now she looked at the fruit with her mind's eye, and seeing with the mind's eye breeds desire. Eve was not careful to filter the images that permeated her mind, a lesson we all can learn. If we like what we see, what we see is what we will want.

The third lust, or temptation, was the pride of life. God knows the difference between good and evil, and the serpent apparently did also. Therefore, why shouldn't she? When all other temptations fail, this one rarely does. It fuels our love of self and pursuit of power and self-glorification. Eve saw no problem with being equal with God. By this point, sin seemed worth the cost. Entertaining sin has a way of destroying one's spiritual capacity for reason.

Thus, prudence says to guard your mind and quickly dismiss the desire to entertain sin. Because conception leads to destruction, our imagination will devise a plan, and Satan will provide the opportunity.

You First

> And Adam was not deceived, but the woman being deceived was in the transgression.
> 1 Timothy 2:14

Sin is not naturally solo; it affects two or more persons. When it doesn't, the person committing the sin usually attempts to recruit others. Every alcoholic I've encountered proved to be quite benevolent when it came to sharing a drink with friends. Unwed sex affects at least two people. Scientists have proposed that abusing drugs can lead to affiliation with drug-abusing peers (NIDA 2003). Like a virus, this is how sin sustains itself; reproduction is the key to survival.

Eve, like a drug pusher, gave the fruit to Adam. The Bible records that Eve did all the talking, but looking closely at the text, we see that Adam was "with her." How many times do we allow others to sin without saying a word? "Not my business," we say. Have you ever considered why the serpent tempted Eve instead of Adam, especially since Adam was with her? Perhaps the innocence of children can provide some insight.

Children have a unique means of exploration. Some are more outgoing than others. Take a trip to a typical playground, and you will most likely see a set of monkey bars or something similar. Climbing the monkey bars, with most children, comes long after the first consideration. The courageous will give it their best effort with blatant disregard for the gravitational consequences feared by on-looking parents. The conservative child will wait until someone else proves the strange playpen can be safely negotiated. The latter appears to have been the character of Adam.

Adam listened to the whole conversation. We don't know if he interjected his thoughts. If he did, God chose not to tell Moses that part of the story – Moses is credited with writing the first five books of the bible. We know that he watched Eve eat the fruit. I can imagine he must have watched her facial expression as she chewed. Her countenance would confirm the value of its taste. I have no doubt that the fruit was pleasing in every way. To the flesh, sin usually is. Now that the monkey bars had been safely negotiated, Adam was ready to give it a go.

Adam made a conscious decision to eat the fruit; he did not recklessly rush in. No, he was not deceived (1 Timothy 2:14). I heard a preacher once say that Adam saw his wife eat of the tree and knew that she would die, and his love for her moved him to accept the same fate. That is a very romantic view of the scripture. Only one problem…why would he allow the person he loved so dearly to choose death in the first place? Do we also sit back and watch the people we love do harmful things to themselves yet profess that we love them?

THE FALL OF MAN

Descent of Character

> And the eyes of them both were opened, and
> they knew that they were naked; and they
> sewed fig leaves together, and made
> themselves aprons.
> Genesis 3:7

The fall of man is the primary reason for the broken relationship between God and man. Man's fall meant the descent of his character, his sense of responsibility, and his commitment to righteousness. These three traits are essential to a prosperous relationship with God. After man sinned, his ability to maintain them degraded fast.

"Unto the pure all things are pure…" (Titus 1:15), but when sin entered, Adam and Eve were no longer pure. The first thing to go was their character. They realized that they were exposed and tried to cover themselves. Rather than facing the consequence of sin, they determined that it was better to cover it. Rather than being marked by integrity, doing the right thing when no one is watching, they chose deceit, which is an indicator of questionable character.

Genesis 3:8 tells us that when "they heard the voice of the Lord God walking in the garden in the cool of the day," they ran and hid themselves. Did they think that God was unaware of the extent of their mischief? God called out, "Adam, where are you?" God, with this question, gave Adam the opportunity to repent and take responsibility for his actions. Adam answered, "I heard you and was naked, afraid, and hiding."

Adam did not tell God where he was physically, but he provided a clear indication of where he was spiritually. In particular, the verbs *are* and *was* of the question and answer, respectively, help us see the exchange in a deeper context. As we read in 1 John 4:18, "there is no fear in love; but perfect love casteth out fear: because fear hath torment. He that feareth is not made perfect in love." To love God is to keep His commandments, and Adam left his first love when he chose to disobey his creator. Sin made him feel exposed (naked), and exposure brought about the birth of fear. He was perfect prior to sin but became fearful (afraid) when sin entered. The influence of fear, in shaping Adam's responses, evidenced his betrayal of God's love. He was no longer perfect in love.

Where *was* Adam? He *was* in sin. There is no sin in God; there is only perfection. In godly perfection, there is no fear. So justifiably, by choosing not to abide in the love of God, he *was* no longer perfect; he *was* abiding in fear.

The offspring of fear is insecurity, which drove Adam to hide himself. As common with fear-born insecurity, it leads to questionable character.

16

Fear has a way of overshadowing the things that make us who we are: our hopes, dreams, principles, flaws, and mistakes. Adam emerged from his hiding place but was not willing to voluntarily admit his blunder. Spiritually, he was still hiding.

Nevertheless, Adam was given another chance to confess and save the relationship. In Genesis 3:11, God asked him question number two: "Who told you that you were naked?" Before he could answer, God cut to the heart of the matter. "Hast thou eaten of the tree, whereof I commanded thee that thou shouldest not eat?"

Descent of Responsibility

> And the man said, The woman whom thou
> gavest to be with me, she gave me of the tree,
> and I did eat.
> Genesis 3:12

Adam's attempt to tell the truth once again fell short. He began his reply with the words, "The woman." God wants us to accept the fact that we have sinned and repent. Sin rarely affects one person, but every person makes their own choices. Again, God's question was, "Who told you that you were naked?" We are told that he knew that he was

17

naked because his eyes were opened. So the complete truth was that no one told him he was naked. He discovered his nakedness after he ate from the tree of knowledge.

The second two words in his reply were "thou gavest." With this, he not only implicated Eve in his sin, but also God. This system of blaming others as well as God for our indiscretions is prevalent today. Like Adam, we are quick to relinquish responsibility for our actions. We imply that we would not have failures if we could operate alone and be left to our own devices.

From this came the principle of "*had not, then I would not*." How often we say things like: "if I *had not* grown up in the inner city, *I would not* have committed that crime," or "if my mother *had not* ignored me, *I would not* have taken those drugs," or "if my father *had not* abandoned me, *I would not* have failed at being a father." After all, "if the government *had not* taxed me so much, *I would not* have committed fraud." Adam argued, "If Eve *had not* given me that fruit or if you (God) *had not* given Eve to me, then *I would not* have eaten the fruit." A more responsible Adam would have responded, "If I *had not* disobeyed you, we *could have* avoided this difficult conversation."

Adam, being the leader of this newly formed family, led his spouse into passing the blame. God asked her, "What is this that thou has done?" She, in turn, followed Adam's example. The first words Eve spoke were, "The serpent." God inquired about what she did, but she elected to tell Him what the serpent did. Adam vacated responsibility in his response, which exposed more unintended consequences. His unwillingness to take responsibility for his actions surely beckoned Eve to do the same. Ultimately, this moment marked the entrance of the irresponsible behavior that pervades mankind.

Descent of Righteousness

> So He drove out the man; and he placed at the
> east of the garden of Eden Cherubim, and a
> flaming sword which turned every way, to
> keep the way of the tree of life.
> Genesis 3:24

God expelled Adam and Eve from the Garden of Eden as one of the consequences for their disobedience and deceit. The garden was a place of peace and tranquility made expressly for them. The world that was meant to be their refuge became the place of their interment. They were driven away in shame, failure, and death. It was not enough that God could not trust them to take care of the garden; He could not trust them to leave and never return. Therefore, He commissioned an angel and a flaming sword to ensure they remained out of the Garden of Eden. The way Adam and Eve answered His questions proved that their capacity for righteousness was severely degraded. They were no longer trustworthy.

Honor eluded them, yet in them was life. This life was an eternal spirit, which God breathed into man after He formed him from the dust of the earth (Genesis 2:7). The flesh, being temporal, was perfect (without sin), but it was not inherently eternal. This was God's beautiful design. Before man sinned, God already had a plan to restore him, and the tree of life and the tree of knowledge were integral parts of His restoration strategy. We will revisit these trees later in the chapter, further examining their respective roles in the fall and redemption of mankind.

CONSEQUENCE OF SIN

A World in Distress

> For the earnest expectation of the creature
> waiteth for the manifestation of the sons of
> God. For the creature was made subject to
> vanity, not willingly...Because the creature
> itself also shall be delivered from the bondage
> of corruption into the glorious liberty of the
> children of God.
> Romans 8:19-21

God gave man dominion over the earth, and his sin introduced suffering to everything subject to his authority. Like a servant under a cruel master, the earth was now subject to the rule of a being that lacked character, responsibility, and righteousness. Creation – the creature in the above scripture – now waits for the end of man's reign, a ruler that hunts animals for sport, strips the land of its resources, and destroys habitats. Conservationists try to prevent this destructive behavior; but, ironically, these activities have long been viewed as the price of advancing civilization. Modernization requires resources, resources that man needs but cannot create. Man has the ability to dream, but he has to exploit God's creation to make his dreams come true.

Creation anticipates freedom from its corrupt dominator. We experience earthquakes, tornadoes, and hurricanes as an indirect result of human sin. These phenomena are often referred to as "acts on God," but I doubt He is so involved. God twisted the world on its axis, and balanced it to spin perpetually. He intervenes at appropriate times, but climate changes and devastations are the natural consequences of death. Creation is aging as man ages. The earth aches with the pains of corruption, and we compound her pain by mismanaging her resources. The planet, therefore, "groaneth and travaileth in pain" (Romans 8:22). It awaits the restoration of peace, which comes with Christ's return.

A Son in Distress

> Wherefore, as by one man sin entered into the world, and death by sin; and so death passed upon all men, for that all have sinned:
> Romans 5:12

The repercussions of Adam's sin were far-reaching. Man has to endure spiritual and natural devastation. Our spirits are pure because they are born of God, yet we have a natural tendency towards sin because we are born of our ancestors. This is the never-ending threat of sin. Sin evolves through our imagination and reproduces through our seed.

Cain and Abel, the sons of Adam and Eve, were victims of Adam's sin. The Bible records in Genesis 4, "that Cain brought of the fruit of the ground an offering unto the Lord." Cain's offering seems to have been one of little consideration. The Bible is not very descriptive in explaining Cain's offering. God took great care to say, however, that Abel "brought of the firstlings of his flock and of the fat thereof" (v. 4). The fact that Abel's sacrifice was of the firstlings and the fattest suggests that he gave God his best, which pleased the Lord.

Cain's actions indicated that the decline of Adam's character, responsibility, and righteousness was passed on to the next generation. Although his sacrifice was not accepted, God tried to restore him and teach him how to be a respectable man, a man of great *character*. God, in a fatherly way, counseled him that righteousness yields acceptance (v. 7).

A man of *righteousness* would have admitted his sin and his anger, but Cain had another option in mind – he chose to kill his brother. When God asked,

"Where is Abel thy brother?" (Genesis 4:9), Cain demonstrated the decline in accepting *responsibility*. He lied and said he didn't know – he actually killed Able. Then, he performed a diversionary tactic and asked his own question, "Am I my brother's keeper?" Prior to this event, the seed of sin within man only exhibited disobedience and deceit. Now, there was murder.

With each new sin, the world became more sinful until God enlisted Noah to build an Ark for the safety of His elect, and the death spiral continues to this day. With every wicked act, sin is added to our seed and passed to our children. Thus, children desire things they have never experienced. For instance, children have a natural tendency to lie and steal (Leach 2002). Mankind, from one generation to the next, perpetuates the death spiral; and Cain, by murdering his brother, has the dubious distinction of being the first to experience the power of sin to affect successive generations.

Every person born from the seed of Adam suffers from the curse of sin, but God promised, in Jeremiah 31:31, that a new covenant with the houses of Israel and Judah was forthcoming. His new covenant would relieve the distress of sin. We would no longer be held accountable for the sins of our fathers. This covenant would break the curse of sin and mend the relationship destroyed by sin.

DESIGNED FOR REDEMPTION

The Inherent Pursuit

> And the LORD God formed man of the dust of the ground, and breathed into his nostrils the breath of life; and man became a living soul.
> Genesis 2:7

Man's spirit came from God. It was not created; it was imparted. Our spirits contain the fundamental properties of God himself. The *lust of the flesh* brought about sin not the *lust (desires) of the spirit*. "The spirit desires what is contrary to the flesh" (Galatians 5:17, NIV). Therefore, the righteous desires of the spirit drive humanity to act in virtuous ways, even in the absence of a religious impetus. We often refer to this as our conscience.

It is also the reason most cultures give homage to a god. Sin severed the connection between our spirit and God, which makes us incomplete without Him. In essence, we create gods in an attempt to reconnect with the God from whence we came. This pursuit has brought about African gods, Aztec gods, Asian gods, Egyptian gods, Celtic gods, Roman gods, oceanic gods, earth gods, celestial gods, etc. The fact that the pursuit of God is common among peoples leads us to conclude that our desire to reconnect with the being that is superior to us is inborn.

Almost An Angel

> Thou madest him a little lower than the angels;
> thou crownedst him with glory and honour,
> and didst set him over the works of thy hands:
> Hebrews 2:7

Angels are intelligent beings designed and created by God to serve Him in various capacities. Beyond the obvious differences such as wings (Ezekiel 1:11), man was made without two significant properties that angels possess. First, Ezekiel 28:13 states that Lucifer (or Satan) was "...full of wisdom..." Such wisdom was withheld from man – man was not created with the ability to distinguish good from evil. Second, angels have celestial (eternal) bodies, and man was given a terrestrial (temporal) body (1 Corinthians 15:40).

Hence, it makes sense that man was made "a little lower than the angels" (Hebrews 2:7).

Angels know the difference between right and wrong. They either choose obedience, as in the case of those who fulfill their angelic duties as messengers and servants of God, or they choose defiance, as in the case of Satan. Many scholars have concluded that Ezekiel 28:15-18 is a reference to the fall of Satan. In this passage, Satan became intoxicated by his own beauty and deceived by his own wisdom. Unlike the fall of man, the genesis of his temptation was not external but intrinsic, not unwitting but conscious.

Without the tree of knowledge, Adam and Eve could not distinguish right from wrong. Eating from the tree of knowledge, therefore, could not have been a matter of choosing evil. At worst, it was a lack of trust, and a lack of trust usually brings relationships to an end. After Adam and Eve ate of the tree of knowledge, God "drove out the man; and He placed cherubim at the east of the garden of Eden, and a flaming sword…to keep the way of the tree of life" (Genesis 3:24). Their disobedience signaled to God that they could not be trusted to keep His commandment. In particular, they were not likely to keep a commandment to stay out of the garden, so He put a measure in place to keep them out.

Note that they were not driven out of the garden because they sinned but to prevent their access to tree of life. They were now as God, knowing good and evil. God, however, purposed not to allow them to eat of the tree of life and live forever (Genesis 3: 22). Eating from the tree of knowledge was a big deal, but eating from the tree of life was detrimental to God's plan.

Initially, God placed the eternal properties of man's body in the tree of life, which was also in the middle of the garden. Just as eating from the tree of knowledge added to man's consciousness the knowledge of good and evil, eating from the tree of life would have added to his body the property of eternal life. This would have put man in the same state as Satan, eternally lost. God allowed man to physically die yet maintained the opportunity to save his soul.

Angels are spirit beings that lack a temporal body. Thus, Satan and the fallen angels were without a means of restoration after sin entered the angelic ranks. Their eternal bodies were eternally corrupted. When that which is eternal is corrupted, it is eternally so. Consider Jesus. He came in the form of man to die for our sins. It was necessary for Him to bear our sins in a corruptible body so He could shed our sins during the resurrection and put on a glorified body. It is this glorified, eternal body that allows Him to be our eternal hope.

Preventing Adam from eating from the tree of life preserved him and mankind until God's plan of salvation could be enacted. God knew that once man sinned, he would do it again. Nevertheless, the grace, mercy, and love of God would not leave us without a means of redemption. God deferred eternal death until He could fulfill his plan to offer eternal life to the world.

Chapter 2

SALVATION DEFINED

Who delivered us from so great a death, and
doth deliver: in whom we trust that he will yet
deliver us;
2 Corinthians 1:10

After God made man in His image, He noted
that the whole of creation was very good
(Genesis 1:31). Adam, made in the image of God,
allowed sin to disfigure his perfect reflection. Hence,
Jesus said that there is none good but God
(Mark 10:18). Now that God's reflection in the earth
is tainted, God stands alone in His corrupt-free
goodness. The first defining moment in man's
history points to the garden where he initially sinned,
which led to the dismantling of humanity's way of
life and the devastation of the planet over which
Adam had been given dominion. Thankfully, God

did not leave His image without the hope of restoration. He instituted the plan of salvation.

Salvation can be and has been defined in many different ways. Among them, three stand out as the most comprehensive and functional. First, salvation can be defined as the deliverance from the power, penalty, and presence of sin. To receive salvation is to receive God's mercy and His grace. Banishment to Hell, which is the ultimate penalty of sin, is scratched from the future of those who receive His gift of eternal life. Salvation restores self-control and discipline to the life of a person, which was once controlled by emotions and self-desire. Temperance can only be realized when sin is rendered impotent, and that is exactly what salvation does.

Second, salvation can be described as a finished work, an on-going work, and a work to come. It is a finished work because Christ died once to bear the sins of humanity. "It is finished," He cried while nailed to a cross – the Roman's contemporary vehicle of choice to expedite ones journey towards death. It is an on-going work because He is continuously conforming us to His image and working to maintain our relationship with

Him. Christians anticipate the day of perfection, when He shall appear without warning and "unto them that look for Him shall He appear the second time without sin unto salvation" (Romans 9:28). That great day will be the culmination of salvation, the work to come, for those who believe and receive the gift of eternal life through Jesus Christ.

Third, salvation can be simply defined as a salvaging process. When people salvage something, they take what is perceived to be useless and transform it into something of great value. As a child growing up in Houston, I can remember my brother and his friends taking what seemed to be good for nothing bicycle frames and making bicycles that were better than new.

First, they would burn the bicycle frames to remove the old paint and prepare them for vigorous sanding. After they were sanded, the frames were painted. They took very special care not to over spray, which would leave streaks. Streaks would constitute redoing the whole process. Finally, with an assortment of seat, handlebar, tire, and rim combinations, they designed each bike as uniquely as they could. They never built a bike the same way twice.

Salvation is God's salvaging process. After the fall of man, humanity was destined to spend eternity wasting away in Hell. We were truly worthless, but God could still see masterpieces. He took us from the garbage heaps of life with a deliberate plan for our restoration.

Sometimes the burning and sanding, our trials and tribulation, are measures He uses to prepare us for His covering, which prevents us from rusting away. As He beautifies us, He warns us against pride, the undesirable streaks in His masterpiece. Finally, He designs us according to His will. No two people are designed the same. All are unique, special, and made (saved) for a specific purpose (1 Corinthians 12:18).

Salvation describes the believer's deliverance from sin, God's life-altering work, and the redemptive process. This chapter expands on these ideas by carefully examining four terms intimately related to God's plan of salvation:

justification, regeneration, sanctification, and glorification.

Justification deals with the penalty of sin; regeneration, the pleasure of sin; sanctification, the power of sin; and glorification, the presence of sin. These four terms also represent salvation's completed work, on-going work, and work to come. Together, they cast light on the salvaging process. To understand these terms is to understand salvation.

JUSTIFICATION

And such were some of you: but ye are
washed, but ye are sanctified, but ye are
justified in the name of the Lord Jesus, and by
the Spirit of our God.
1 Corinthians 6:11

Romans 5:6-10 is a compelling passage of scripture as it relates to God's love expressed through salvation. Paul points out that we were without strength before the sacrifice of Jesus Christ. We were incapable of saving ourselves and were powerless to overcome the desires of our flesh, but in due time (at the right time) Jesus died to receive us unto Himself and save us from a certain damnation. This deed was an enormous expression of love.

Romans 5:7 says, "scarcely for a righteous man will one die: yet peradventure for a good man some would even dare to die." In essence, we may consider dying for a good friend or a family member or even volunteer to die for a noble person who has done great deeds within our community or a person we deem to be a hero. To die for an enemy, on the other hand, is almost unthinkable.

I have three sons, and I cannot fathom a situation where I would allow them to die to save someone else – especially a disloyal person. The crucifixion and subsequent death of Jesus is the greatest testimony of God's love for humanity. We, like Adam, disregard God's commandments and seek our own way, prioritizing personal pursuits above our relationship with Him. Even so, "while we were yet sinners, Christ died for [all of] us" (Romans 5:8) to wash, sanctify, and justify us by the Spirit of God (1 Corinthians 6:11).

Through The Blood

> Moreover he sprinkled with the blood both the
> tabernacle, and all the vessels of the ministry.
> And almost all things are by the law purged
> with blood; and without shedding of blood is
> no remission.
> Hebrews 9:21-22

The law of remission of or release from sin requires that almost all things be cleansed by a blood sacrifice (Hebrews 9:22). Romans 4:25 proclaims that Jesus "was delivered for our offences and was raised again for our justification." Our sins were remitted at Jesus' death. In His death, we are declared just. Such a justification, in the same manner as the blood of bulls and goats (Hebrews 10: 1-4), is momentary. Romans 4:25 points to the resurrection of Christ as the necessary element to make our atonement eternal.

A detailed explanation of the importance of His resurrection and its impact on our eternal redemption can be found in the 9th and 10th chapters of Hebrews. In summary, the high priest of the Old Testament made daily sacrifices and went into the Holy of Holies once per year to make atonement for his and the people's sins. The resurrected Christ, being our high priest, by His own blood obtain our eternal redemption once for all.

Faith and/or Works

Paul says in the 4th chapter of Romans that Abraham was counted just because he believed God and not because of his works. In verse 5, he says, "to him that worketh not, but believeth on Him that justifieth the ungodly, his faith is counted unto him as righteousness without works." Paul highlights the weakness of our works in securing salvation. Salvation is an act of God's grace.

Paul cautions the church at Ephesus that "by grace are ye saved through faith; and not of yourselves: it is a gift of God: not of works, lest any man should boast" (Ephesians 2:8-9). If our best deeds are said to be as filthy rags (Isaiah 64:6), then our feeble attempts to justify ourselves before God are futile. Paul attributes total credit and responsibility to God for our justification.

In the book of James, we discover an apparent disagreement with Paul's doctrine of works-free justification. James 2:14 asked the question, "Can faith alone save us?" We need look no further than the next twelve verses to answer the question. James holds that faith without works is dead, useless. This idea is repeated several times within the chapter.

He presses his claim as though he is engaged in a strong debate. First, he suggests that it is not enough to simply say we have faith. If we say we have faith and fail to help the less fortunate, our faith is dead (vv. 14-17). Second, works are a demonstration of faith. James proposes that he shows his faith by his works. Furthermore, Abraham, by his faith, offered Isaac as a sacrifice, and Rahab, by faith, hid the messengers of Israel at Jericho. Abraham and Rahab were justified by their works and not by faith alone (vv. 18-25). Third, he compares faith and works to life itself. As the body dies without the spirit, faith is dead without works (v. 26).

Should we agree with James or Paul? Many have waged their own debate over which doctrine is correct.

"All scripture is given by inspiration of God, and is profitable for doctrine..." (2 Timothy 3:16). Therefore, we must conclude that Paul and James were correct in their analysis of works as it relates to our justification. It is clear that Paul and James wrote about different kinds of work. Furthermore, we find three distinct linkages between works and justification: works of justification, works that follow justification, and works that justify.

Works of justification are works done to befriend God or excuse our wretchedness in His sight. Paul speaks strongly against these works. To understand his objection to these works, we must keep in mind that he was writing to a community containing Jews that did not believe Jesus was the Messiah. After reading Romans 3, we learn that he was addressing works of justification (the Law).

Many believers, at the time, were demanding that the Gentiles receive the rite of circumcision to obtain proper fellowship with God. They were disregarding the saving power of God though faith in Jesus and replaced a spiritual relationship with physical actions. In essence, they attended church every week as a way of paying a debt of time or gave money to the church to fulfill an obligation to perform a good deed. These are modern-day examples of the circumcision Paul advised against.

Works of justification are physical acts done in the hope that they will make us pure in God's eyes and prevent us from being cast into hell. To reason that benevolent people or people who have lived a good life should be allowed in heaven leads to a faulty assertion. One can neither work their way in or out of heaven. Circumcision, physical or otherwise, stands powerless to justify us before God.

Works that follow justification are characterized by a sincere love and commitment towards God. These works are not easily distinguishable from works of justification. The difference is found in the motive of the heart and the intent of the mind. After justification, church services become worship services and are attended in response to a sincere love for God and His people.

The believer no longer attends worship service because it is a longstanding family ritual. A strong desire to know more about God's word surfaces. Bible study is added to the weekly list of things to do. Tithes and offerings are given without regard to what God will do in return. The only concern becomes the prosperity of God's work and His will.

After justification, the circumcision can fulfill its true purpose (Romans 4:10-11). We begin to cut away things to exemplify our covenant with God. We begin to remove words from our vocabulary, articles from our wardrobe, and less desirable habits. All that is done, is done to the Glory of God.

God chose the circumcision to "be a token of the covenant" between Him and Abraham (Genesis 17: 9-11). Believers must be careful to remember with Whom they have their covenant. The tokens God chooses for us can serve as evidence of our justification; they can never be the source of our justification. If we pursue the tokens God has chosen for others, then we are increasing the potential for our works to become works of justification.

This is not to say that we should never participate in the tokens of other believers. At times, it is beneficial for believers to join together in a common, covenant token. God commanded Moses to pass his token on to his children (Genesis 17:10). Likewise, if God gives the leader of His people a token to be honored by the people, then it becomes the responsibility of the people to participate in the keeping of that token where possible. The most important thing to remember is that the token does not justify. It is only a physical display of one's covenant with God.

It may seem a contradiction to say that works cannot justify and then say there are works that justify. Just as "faith," a noun, cannot produce a sentence or a complete thought without a verb, James stressed that faith without works is useless. He goes on to say that the devils believe that there is one God and tremble, suggesting that simply believing there is a God is not enough (James 2:19). There must be works involved. What are these works? Let's consider them works of faith, works that provide evidence of our faith in God.

Paul explained the way to obtain salvation in Romans 10:9-10:

> 9. That if thou shalt confess with thy mouth the Lord Jesus, and shalt believe in thine heart that God has raised him from the dead, thou shalt be saved.
> 10. For with the heart man believeth unto righteousness; and with the mouth confession is made unto salvation.

When we believe, a verb, and confess that God raised Jesus from the dead, we demonstrate our trust in the Lord. Our confession is a work of faith. This work must take place. Without it, we cannot be justified before God.

Abraham believed God, but his belief was evidenced by his willingness to sacrifice his son Isaac. Likewise, confession completes our faith. We can believe that Jesus was and is the Son of God. We can also believe He died and was raised from the grave. We cannot, however, expect to benefit from these facts until we confess Him as Lord and enter into a covenant relationship with Him. This is the only acceptable work in the process of justification. Once this work is complete, works of love and commitment will follow.

REGENERATION

Regeneration brings about a vast improvement in the life of the believer through a God-orchestrated rebirth. This is the recycling element of salvation. Those who volunteer for the process are reproduced from the inside out. "Old things are passed away; behold, all things are become new" (2 Corinthians 5:17). No faction is left untouched. Internally, we experience a new birth, and externally, we experience a new life.

Rebirth

Jesus told Nicodemus, in John chapter 3, that a man must be born again to enter the kingdom of God. He cautioned him that being born of the water (natural birth) is simply not enough to gain access into the kingdom, or rule, of God. We must be born again – born of the Spirit. This rebirth is paramount in the process of regeneration.

Regeneration of the Spirit is not something man can control. It is an act of God, only received through the Spirit upon our obedience to the truth (1 Peter 1:23). The Spirit of God brings our dead spirit to life when the incorruptible seed, the word, is planted in our hearts. This new life is expressed in a newfound relationship with God.

In Romans 12:2, we are challenged not to conform to this world but to be transformed. The difference between conforming to this world and being transformed is an important distinction to understand. Conformance takes place without changing substance or composition. When water is poured into a glass, it conforms to the shape of the glass.

Paul, by using the word "conform," suggested that believers should not take the shape of the world. When we conform to the world, we imitate, mimic, act like, speak like, and think like the world. The world will attempt to shape our responses, attitudes, and postures by suggesting that we conform to its moral ideologies, methodologies, and standards. Believers and the standards that govern our lives are in constant jeopardy of being reshaped by secular ways of thinking.

The mind controls every function of the human body. It is responsible for the movement of our limbs, the activation of our senses, emotions, and expressions. Therefore, our actions will not change until our minds are changed.

We become what/who we are told we are. If a child is constantly told that he/she is intelligent, then that child will take on difficult challenges believing that success is achievable. Conversely, a child consistently told that he/she is stupid and lazy will likely avoid difficult tasks in fear of failure. The latter rarely, if ever, reaches their potential because they only do enough to get by. Hope can be restored, but it takes the influence of a caring person to change their mind.

Unlike conformation, transformation is a complete alteration. When a caterpillar emerges from its cocoon, it does so as a butterfly. It no longer walks long distances. It flies. It can never return to being a caterpillar. So it is with Christians; our transformation is conclusive.

We cannot return to the life of a caterpillar once the process of salvation begins. As we hide ourselves in the cocoon of His Word and the fellowship of His Spirit, the inward change becomes externally expressed. Things can never be the way they were after enlightenment.

What about blasphemy you may ask? How does it impact one's salvation? First, let's clarify what blasphemy does not mean. Blasphemy is not synonymous with backsliding. A backslider experiences the truth, obeys the truth, turns from the truth, but maintains that God is truth. A blasphemer experiences the truth, obeys the truth, turns from the truth, and denounces that God is truth. To blaspheme, the believer must denounce the existence of God and accept eternal damnation. The book of Hebrews addresses this:

> For it is impossible for those who were once enlightened, and have tasted of the heavenly gift, and were made partakers of the Holy Ghost, And have tasted the good word of God, and the powers of the world to come, If they should fall away, to renew them again unto repentance; seeing they crucify to themselves the Son of God afresh, and put him to an open shame.
> Hebrews 6:4-6

Taking this passage literally, we determine that the audience here are believers. The persons discussed "were made partaker of the Holy Ghost," and the ministry of the Holy Ghost is exclusively a Christian experience.

The challenge before us is to address the age-old question and validity of eternal security. This is an argument I gave up a long time ago. I could compile scripture and spin them to support both for and against. Although we address the subject in more detail in Chapter 8, the question is among the least debate-worthy subjects in scripture. It is far more important for believers to help the world experience the rebirth we've come to know.

Personally, it is difficult to imagine someone getting to know God through the baptism of His Spirit then deciding to willingly work against Him. The Bible, however, warns against making such a choice. Those who blasphemed against God in the Old Testament were provided redemption through the promise of the Messiah, Jesus Christ. Those who blasphemed against Jesus were redeemed through the promise of the baptism of the Holy Ghost. God has not made a promise of redemption for those who blaspheme against the Holy Ghost.

Whether our salvation is eternal or not, through it we obtain new life. Recall from Chapter 1 that man was forbidden to eat from the tree of life and was expelled from the Garden of Eden to prevent him from doing so in a corrupt state. Humanity remained unrighteous but not for eternity.

Jesus became our sacrifice for sin and restored us to a place of righteousness. Although Adam could not eat of the tree of life, we are granted this privilege through Jesus Christ. He said He is the tree of life. When we accept Christ, we gain a new life in Him. We experience a glorious new birth where sin no longer separates us from the love of God. The past, present, and future sins of those born of the Spirit are cleansed by the blood of Jesus.

New Life

Rebirth brings "sonship," and with sonship comes a new citizenship. The believer's rebirth is also a heavenly birth, which changes the believer's home of record. We "are no more strangers and foreigner, but fellow citizens with the saints and are of the household of God" (Ephesians 2:19). If a child is born in the United States, he/she has automatic citizenship and is subject to all state and national laws. Christians, being born of heaven, are subject to the laws of Heaven and the Kingdom (rule) of God. We remain bound to the natural laws of this world but are spiritually free.

"Now then we are ambassadors for Christ...," Paul wrote in 2 Corinthians 5:20. We are in this world to speak on Heaven's behalf. Certain laws of this foreign land do not apply to us. While those whose spirits are bound to this world are subject to laws of sin and death, we are not subject to them. As ambassadors for Christ, we have "diplomatic immunity." The world sins and receives the penalty of death. Christians sin and receive the grace of God and the gift of life.

No true, born again or regenerated Christian abuses this privilege by practicing sin. However, after living in a country for an extended period, strangers often lose the accent of their native dialect. This is easily fixed with a quick trip home where one's dialect is common. Thus, it is imperative for the ambassadors of Christ to return "home" through prayer, Bible study, meditation, and praise. Daily communication with Heaven and fellow believers regenerates our mind and helps maintain the language and culture of our spiritual home.

The regeneration of the mind follows the regeneration of the Spirit and the regeneration of our actions follows the regeneration of our mind, which adds up to a new life in Christ. Regeneration brings about a spiritual rebirth through the power of the Holy Ghost. Spiritual rebirth is the gateway to salvation and the prelude to sanctification.

SANCTIFICATION

Our New Place Among Men

> Jude, the servant of Jesus Christ, and brother
> of James, to them that are sanctified by God
> the Father, and preserved in Jesus Christ, and
> called:
> Jude 1:1

Salvation is God's progressive work. Jude, in the verse above, identified his readers first as those sanctified by God the Father. When a person is sanctified, they are set aside – separated from the common and placed among the select. God, through sanctification, separates Christians from the world. "You are a chosen generation," according to 1 Peter 2:9, "to Him who hath called you out of darkness."

After sanctification, Jude identified his readers as preserved in Jesus Christ. Webster defines preserve as follows:

1. To keep safe, as from injury or peril.
2. To maintain unchanged.
3. To keep or maintain intact.

Employing this definition, it follows that we are kept safe, as from injury or peril in Jesus Christ. At salvation, the Spirit of God baptizes us into the body of Christ. From that point on, He works to ensure that our salvation stays intact.

When we are tempted, the Spirit of God charges us to take the way of peace and spiritual prosperity. He moves us to study and meditate on God's word and reminds us of those words when we face trials and tribulations (John 14:26). Jesus moves us to pray and prays for us when we don't know what to say (Romans 8:26). He is a vital part of the longevity of our salvation. Although our trials and tribulations are difficult to bear, He makes sure that they do not destroy us. Therefore, if we listen and obey, we can rest assured that the status of our sanctification will remain unchanged.

The Calling

Finally, his salutation includes those who are called. Everyone in the body of Christ has a calling, but God calls those who are sanctified and preserved. One's calling is a unique responsibility in the Kingdom of God. When God calls us, He is simply giving us permission to fulfill our responsibility. Our calling is our ultimate purpose in life, and it was forged through the foreknowledge of God, prior to our earthly conception. This is what is referred to as predestination, which we examine in greater detail in Chapter 6. To get a better idea of one's calling, let's look at the calling of Moses.

Although the Egyptian pharaoh declared that every male child be put to death, God preserved Moses in the pharaoh's palace. After Moses discovered who he was, he was exiled from his Egyptian family and their way of life. His exile served as his sanctification. The desert was brutal, but God preserved him. He would not allow Moses to die until his purpose was fulfilled.

Why didn't God call him in Egypt? If Moses was destined to stand against Egypt, the Egypt in him had to be filtered out. He needed enough time away from the Egyptian way of life to liberate his mind. Returning to Egypt to confront pharaoh too soon could have led to a situation where he lacked the strength to resist the temptation to stay. Perhaps those who remained in Egypt, such as the elders, would not have been so eager to accept a deliverer who was a recent murderer or who, in custom, was more Egyptian than Hebrew.

Paul told Timothy that bishops should not be novices (1 Timothy 3:6). A person not far removed from the world, could return to the world to set the captives free but find themselves in a position where they aren't strong enough to resist the temptation to stay. Perhaps even those who are in the world, people they are so desperately trying to set free, will not be so eager to accept a spiritual leader who is still secular in thought, mannerisms, and deeds. Not to disparage the calling of any, but pastors and overseers, like Moses, are most effective when they are sanctified and preserved to lead God's people.

Taking a closer look, we discover nine important elements of Moses' calling (Exodus 3:1-12):

He was watchful. Moses was pre-occupied with his sheep, but he noticed the burning bush (v. 2). When the normal activities of life arrest our focus, we should remain watchful and cognizant that God may be working to get our attention. Tunnel vision limits our field of view and can cause us to miss the signs God erects to call us towards the next step in our destiny.

He turned aside to see. Moses realized that the burning bush was a supernatural phenomenon, so he put aside his agenda to seek an explanation of what he saw (v. 3). The call of God demands a willingness to put aside our agenda when He interrupts our activities and plans.

His calling only came after he turned aside (v. 4). One's calling is based on the ability to say nevertheless, thy will be done (Luke 22:42) and put aside self-will for the will of God.

Moses was ordered to show humility (v. 5). God instructed him to take off his shoes – a demonstration of respect and honor towards God. Although we can go boldly before the throne of God, it is imperative that we remember that His very existence and glory merits our humility.

God introduced Himself to Moses (v 6.). Moses was called to be God's ambassador. Every ambassador should be familiar with the authority they represent. When speaking for God or acting on His behalf – as all Christian do – we represent the highest authority and should seek first a proper introduction.

God explained the purpose of Moses' calling (v. 7). God uses people to accomplish earthly tasks. God's calling *on* us is not *for* us. He calls us to assist and bring about a change in the life of others. He uses those he calls to answer the prayers of those who call on Him.

God gave the specifics of Moses' calling (v. 10). God told Moses exactly what He wanted done, but He did not tell him how to do it. The "how" usually comes in the process of fulfilling the call. Our success depends on our faith in God, and the less we know the more we are required to trust.

Moses expressed his inadequacies (v. 11). Moses realized he couldn't fulfill his calling alone. God does not call us based on our abilities; no one has the natural ability to fulfill God's calling within themselves. As with Moses, God fulfills the calling not *by* us but *through* us.

God promised not to leave Moses alone (v. 12). No matter how big the task, we must remember that God will always be with us, and He will ensure our success. Therefore, serving the people of God must begin and end with serving the God of the people.

The Empowerment

> For this is the will of God, even your
> sanctification, that ye should abstain from
> fornication. That every one of you should
> know how to possess his vessel in
> sanctification and honour;
> 1 Thessalonians 4:3-4

Our sanctification is the will of God. He sanctifies us as well as empowers us to discipline ourselves. We are given the power required to live separate and distinct from the world. He gives us victory over sin and empowers us to sanctify ourselves unto Him and His work. Sanctification is a charge from God to exercise the power that is within us to live according to the will of God and abstain from sin.

Jude 1:21 says to "Keep yourselves in the love of God..." What a great task, which rests upon every believer? God sanctifies through His love, and Jude declares that the maintenance of that sanctification belongs to the believer. Those who are sanctified through the love of God should strive daily to ensure that their actions are consistent with His love.

Believers must remain conscious of their spiritual sanctification as well as their physical sanctification. The Lord, in the words of Paul, challenges us to "come out from among them, and be ye separate, saith the Lord, and touch not the unclean thing; and I will receive you" (2 Corinthians 6:17). We must, at all times, "walk worthy of the Lord unto all pleasing, being fruitful in every good work, and increasing in the knowledge of God" (Colossians 1:10).

Pleasing God should be paramount; it should be the most important aspiration of those who believe in Christ. How do we please God? Colossians 1:10 says that we please the Lord by being fruitful in every good work and by increasing in the knowledge of God. Reading the next verse (v. 11), we also discover that being fruitful and growing in the knowledge of God strengthens the believer and manifests the godly attributes of sanctification.

The eighth chapter of Romans is rich with doctrinal truths that are arguably the most empowering concepts contained in scripture. In Romans 7, Paul describes the human struggle, a war of righteousness against sin that seems unwinnable. In Romans 8, however, he paints a picture of victory.

Although the flesh (human desires) cannot please God (Romans 8:8), we do not have to live after (obey) the flesh (Romans 8:12). In fact, the Spirit of God empowers us to mortify the deeds of our body (Romans 8:13). This power gives us the ability to discipline ourselves, which connotes discipleship. To whatever extent possible, the actions of Christ's disciples should never be found in contradiction to their spiritual sanctification.

GLORIFICATION

That might present it to himself a glorious church, not having spot, or wrinkle, or any such thing; but that it should be holy and without blemish.
Ephesians 5:27

Justification, regeneration, and sanctification are opening acts to God's completed work, our perfection. Salvation begins with our faith and ends in perfection. Upon the proclamation of our faith, Jesus justifies us before the Father; the Father sanctifies us according to His will; the Holy Spirit regenerates us; and we become the children of God. The Father, Son, and the Holy Spirit work together for the common goal of producing a glorious church.

Romans 8:30 states that we are predestined, called, justified, and glorified (translated from the Greek word doxazo, rendered excellent). Ultimately, God desires to present us to Himself as a glorious church at the return of Christ. This will be the culmination of our transformation, the completed work of salvation.

According to 1 Corinthians 15, we will be changed when Christ returns for us. Paul tells us in verse 49 that we now bear the image of the earthly (Adam), but we will also bear the image of the heavenly (Jesus). We know that Jesus, after His resurrection, received a glorified body. Likewise, as stated in 1 John 3:2, "It doth not yet appear what we shall be: but we know that, when He shall appear, we shall be like him…" While the internal change has already taken place in the believer's heart and soul, Christ's return will usher in the moment when our external (physical) bodies will be rendered excellent (glorified).

We will be change; our corruptible bodies will become incorruptible; our mortal bodies will become immortal. Sickness and disease will no longer plague us. Handicaps and hard times will fail to persist. Death and decay, which inflicts us all, will cease to be the inevitable outcome of our existence.

We will finally transcend the natural world and live according to the laws of the Spirit. As Paul wrote to the Thessalonians, "We which are alive and remain shall be caught up together with [the dead in Christ] in the clouds, to meet the Lord in the air" (1 Thessalonians 4:17). Our glorified bodies will defy the laws of gravity. Gravity will lose its hold as our external body joins our internal spirit in the glory of perfection.

Chapter 3

COVENANT OF LOVE

Since the fall of man, God has worked diligently to restore the broken relationship with humanity through several carefully planned covenants. These covenants can be placed in one of two categories. They are either covenants of sacrifice or covenants of love. We will focus our attention on two covenants in particular. The first is a foreshadowing of the second.

TWO COVENANTS – ONE PURPOSE

> But he who was of the bondwoman was born after the flesh; but he of the freewoman was by promise. Which things are an allegory: for these are the two covenants...
> Galatians 4: 23-24

There were many covenants made in the Old Testament and New Testament, but none are more significant than God's covenant with Abraham and His covenant extension for the Gentiles, salvation as previously defined in Chapter 2. Why the Abrahamic Covenant? Why not the Mosaic Law? The Abrahamic Covenant was the first covenant with salvation as its eternal reward. The Mosaic Law was a covenant between Israel and God. It was limited in scope because it was given to the Jews alone.

Neither the covenant extension (salvation by grace) nor the covenant with Israel (Mosaic Law) could be realized without Abraham's covenant. Abraham's covenant with God was very similar to the covenant extended to the Gentiles. Both covenants are covenants of sacrifice and both have distinct initiators, composers, and endorsers.

Covenant of Sacrifice

Genesis 15 gives a description of the covenant made between God and Abram, whose name was eventually changed to Abraham. Here, God told Abraham that He would multiply his seed to equal the measure of the stars. He initiated the covenant process by giving Abraham a detailed description of what sacrifices to make and how to prepare them. Abraham simply followed the instructions.

Covenant of Love

John 3:16 best describes God's covenant extension as presented in the New Testament, Matthew through Revelation. It begins with "For God so loved the world." This new covenant is an extension of Abraham's covenant. God chose to make a covenant with Abraham because he was faithful. Now, God has extended the promises of Abraham to those who exercise the faith required to be named among the "whosoever believeth in him." The Abrahamic covenant was governed by Abraham's obedience, but God's covenant with the followers of Christ is governed by His love.

THE COVENANT PROCESS

The table below shows the parallels between the Abrahamic covenant and the covenant extended to whosoever believes in the death, burial, and resurrection of Jesus Christ. It is broken into four distinct phases. Within each phase, there is an initiator, composer, and endorser(s). God is the initiator of both covenants. After all, we cannot come to God (Jesus) unless we are first drawn of the Father (John 6:44). As the initiator of the covenant, God also dictated the terms of the covenant. He chose who would compose it and who would seal it. Finally, a covenant depends on both parties keeping their promises until a better covenant supersedes or fulfills it.

This table compares the covenant between Abram and God and the covenant God shares with all those who believe in His son, Jesus Christ.

The Abrahamic Covenant	The Believer's Covenant
1. God the initiator	1. God the initiator
- God promised a countless inheritance	- God promised eternal life
- God dictated the conditions	- God dictated the conditions
2. Abram the composer	2. God the composer
- Abram prepared the sacrifice	- God prepared the sacrifice
- Abram remembered God's instructions.	- God remembered His prophecies
- Abram followed the instructions	- Jesus fulfilled the prophecies of God
- Abram made a sacrifice of obedience.	- God made a sacrifice of love.
3. God the endorser	3. Believers the endorsers
- God accepted the sacrifice as adequate	- Believers accept the sacrifice as adequate
- His endorsement was His prerogative	- Our endorsement is our prerogative
- God passed through the sacrifice	- We must pass through the sacrifice
- God put himself on the altar	- We are expected to be living sacrifices
4. Abrams covenant relationship	4. Our covenant relationship
- God was faithful to Abram	- God remains faithful to us
- Abram's covenant: founded on obedience	- Believers' covenant is grounded in love
- Abram's obedience released God's favor	- God's love released God's grace
- Faith made Abram a friend of God	- Faith makes believers a child of God

The Initiator

The initiator of both covenants is God. He is the "author and the finisher of our faith" (Hebrews 12:2). In Genesis 13, God reiterated the promise made to Abram in Genesis 12 but with more specificity. The great nation, in chapter 12, which would come from his lineage was likened to the immeasurability of the dust upon which he walked. In Genesis 15, the promise was likened to a lineage that would rival the stars. These descriptions, as grandiose as they were, didn't appear farfetched to Abram. In fact, Abram believed God, and God counted his faith as righteousness, and so began a pattern of faith, works, and revelation.

Abram, at God's word, left Haran with few details. Faith does not required details; it obtains them. Faith is what causes us to trust God at His word and operate in ignorance as though we are fully informed. This unreasonable trust works like a backstage pass, granting access to mysteries that God only shares with the faithful. As the light of day chases away the night with every passing minute, the illumination of God's plan increased with each display of Abram's faith.

God pre-purposed to give Abram the land before Abram left Haran in Genesis 12. After demonstrating his faith by leaving Haran, he obtained clarity in Genesis 13 as to what the "land that I will show you" really meant. While in Canaan, God showed him the land of promise. It was as far northward, southward, eastward, and westward as he could see.

After Abram believed God in Genesis 15, God revealed to him additional details of the promise. The land previously described in general, directional terms was pinpointed between distinguishable boundaries. It lay between the river of Egypt and the river Euphrates. This was an enormous promise, yet Abram believed God and asked for a physical sign to solidify the promise (Genesis 15:8).

The Composer

God didn't simply produce a sign at Abram's request; He made him an active participant. He instructed Abram to get a three-year-old heifer, goat, ram, and a turtledove and young pigeon. Normally, the Levitical order called for animal sacrifices to be one year old (Leviticus 23:19), but these were to be fully mature and undoubtedly *taken* from Abram's flock. They were Abram's contribution to the physical establishment of the covenant. Although

God initiated the covenant, Abram was tasked to compose the sign of the covenant with his own resources.

Abram was given specific instructions, remembered them, and followed them in obedience. Abram thought the words of God to be so significant that He remembered them and accomplished them as stated. He did not deviate. He took three animals from his flock, split them in half, and positioned them along with the two birds, according to God's directions – again showing his faithfulness and obedience.

As with Abram, God answers our prayers and gives us the desires of our heart but not without our active participation. When we do our part in establishing the covenant, we take the verbal agreement and make it tangible. Equally, if not more, important is our obedience in how we demonstrate our faith toward God.

The Endorser

According to Genesis 15:17, God passed between the sacrificial pieces as a smoking furnace and a burning lamp. God's act of passing through the pieces signified that the sacrifice was acceptable. He endorsed the sacrifice with Himself. We read in Hebrews 6:13, "For when God made promise to Abram, because He could swear by no greater, He sware by himself." God put himself on the altar, symbolizing that His fate would follow that of the animals slaughtered if He did not keep His word – a practice recklessly adopted by Judah (Jeremiah 34:18-20).

A covenant is but a promise unless both parties have clearly stated and agreed-upon responsibilities. Generally, each party commits to equitable conditions, but covenants with God are never symmetrical. This is the lesson God wanted the people of Jerusalem to learn in Jerimiah 34. In obedience to the command of God, Zedikiah made a covenant with the people of Jerusalem to proclaim liberty to all the inhabitants thereof (v. 15).

Afterwards, however, they broke the covenant and retrieved those whom they freed to be servants once more (v. 16). God perceived this to be a mockery of His promise of freedom. He applauded their initial obedience but was displeased with the breaking of the covenant they made with their

70

servants and Him. Freeing the servants was a foreshadowing of salvation in that it was an asymmetrical act of grace. The slaves were set free, but they did not earn it nor did they have anything of equal value to give in return for it.

The symbolism of God's plan for our freedom is clear. He provided Himself a sacrifice, the Lamb slain from the foundation of the world, as stated in Revelation 13:8. His sacrifice is the tangible sign of the covenant of salvation, which was composed on the cross at Calvary. He leaves it to us to pass through the sacrifice. Jesus said in John 10:6, "I am the way, the truth, and the life: no man cometh unto the Father, but by me."

By accepting Jesus, we say to God that we are in agreement with the contract sealed with the blood of Jesus Christ and commit to a covenant relationship where the benefit outweighs our contribution. The agreement is binding on God's part to deliver us from sin. In return, He entreats believers to present their bodies as a living sacrifice (Romans 12:1).

THE GIFT OF LOVE

But God commended his love toward us, in
that, while we were yet sinners, Christ died for
us.
Romans 5:8

Ask any Christian if they feel they owe Christ everything and if they feel they are forever indebted to him. They will answer with a resounding "YES!" The person who really understands the sacrifice made for our salvation can come to no other conclusion. Jesus made the ultimate sacrifice, and we who know Him as savior feel an overwhelming desire to show Him our appreciation. From our viewpoint, we owe Him our very lives. However, the problem comes when we begin to think that God has the same perspective. He does not hold us accountable for the debt He paid on our behalf.

No one goes to hell because they refuse to accept Christ as savior. He is not the reason people go to hell. He is the reason people don't go to hell. Without Christ's sacrifice for our sins, we were all destined for hell. His sacrifice provides the means for everyone to redirect their path towards a destiny that culminates in eternal glory and fellowship with the Lord.

God's sacrifice to redeem mankind was an act of love. It was a gift given without our permission or request and offered to mankind without ulterior motives. God simply desires that we show gratitude for His grace by accepting His gift. Upon accepting His gift of life, we enter into a covenant with Him and become free servants of Christ. The covenant, being conceived in love, can only be sustained by love.

Love Me for Me

> We love him, because he first loved us.
> 1 John 4:19

Love screams for reciprocation. Consider a mother's love, the purest example of love. A mother nurtures her children from birth. She feeds and provides for them. She listens intently for their cries and mends their wounds. For all she does, she simply wants a "good morning," an occasional hug, or an "I love you, Mama." The relationship between a mother and her child is rarely characterized by gifts or disappointments. A good mother loves her children regardless of what they do. Although often gone unspoken, her principal desire is for her children to reciprocate her unconditional love.

John encourages the saints in 1 John 4 to love one another unconditionally. His premise for this evocation is the fact that "God is love." Furthermore, we cannot say we are of God if we cannot love the ones we see on a daily basis. Love is an intrinsic quality of the believer. Because God (love) lives in us and we live in Him (love), we are inhabited and engulfed by love.

This love fills our existence, inwardly and outwardly, and goes far beyond a mothers love. This love made the ultimate sacrifice. It expressed itself in an unimaginable way: The Father sent His Son to be the savior of the world (1 John 4:14). Human affection has its limits, but God's love is unconditional and long-suffering. God paid the ultimate price for the forgiveness for our sins. He paid our ransom. What does He want in return? Our love.

Seeking Jesus

> And when they had found [Jesus] on the other
> side of the sea, they said unto him, Rabbi,
> when camest thou hither? Jesus answered them
> and said, Verily, verily, I say unto you, Ye
> seek me, not because ye saw the miracles, but
> because ye did eat of the loaves, and were
> filled. Labour not for the meat which
> perisheth, but for that meat which endureth
> unto everlasting life, which the Son of man
> shall give unto you: for him hath God the
> Father sealed.
> John 6:25-27

This passage refers to the day after Jesus fed over five thousand people with two fish and five pieces of bread. The next day many of the multitude returned to the place where He fed them. They assumed He was where they left Him, on the coast without a boat. After the crowd gathered and found neither Jesus nor His disciples present, they surmised that Jesus must have somehow crossed over to Capernaum. They re-boarded their boats and pursued him.

When the people found Him, they asked, "When comest thou hither?" His mode of travel across the sea must have been a mystery to them, but we know from John 6:19 that He walked on the water part of the way to catch up with the disciples on the ship – the truth would have likely been unbelievable. Nevertheless, Jesus knew they didn't cross the sea to find out how He arrived there and was disappointed with their true motivation. Jesus was not moved nor deceived by their attempt at casual conversation.

There was something different about this group. He was moved with compassion when He fed the multitude with the loaves and fish. Many followed Him for three days, and some among them had a long journey home. His concern for them compelled Him to make provisions for their physical strength. The multitude followed the healer, but this subset of them came for the chef.

They were not looking for Jesus; they were looking for a meal. How easy it is to lose track of what is important. All too often, we take the ones we love for granted – Jesus included. This group allowed the provisions of Jesus to obscure the revelation of God as Jehovah-Jireh, God our provider.

The group of people seeking Jesus gave priority to the meals He provided over the miracles He performed. The meals were temporal, but the miracles pointed to Him as the Messiah, the giver of eternal life. By undervaluing the importance of the miracles, they missed God's evidence of Jesus' true identity and purpose.

The group allowed their blessing to overshadow the importance of the giver, an act not worthy of emulation. We cannot allow the benefits of salvation to overshadow the Savior. The most meaningful miracle is the miracle of salvation...it evidences the miraculous love of God.

When God is the focus of our love, material blessings become additions to, rather than the defining moments of, our relationship with God. A relationship based on love prevents us from blaming Him when things don't happen according to our plan. Whether we lose a family member, develop health problems, or have financial issues, our circumstances can never be used as a measure of God's love for us. He promised never to leave nor forsake us (Hebrews 13:5). His only desire is that we reciprocate. Love Him because He is our God and not because of what He can do for us.

Do You Love Me?

> He saith unto him the third time, Simon, son of
> Jonas, lovest thou me? Peter was grieved
> because he said unto him the third time,
> Lovest thou me? And he said unto him, Lord,
> thou knowest all things; thou knowest that I
> love thee. Jesus saith unto him, Feed my
> sheep.
> John 21:17

Some of Jesus' disciples could not fully accept His teachings and "went back, and walked no more with him. Then said Jesus unto the twelve, 'Will ye also go away?'" (John 6:53-67). They chose to stay. Later, Jesus asked Peter if he loved Him. Then He told him, "Feed my sheep." The emphasis, based on context, was not on the answer but the question, "Do you love me?"

Although Jesus taught Peter about life, earth, and Heaven, provided for him, and mentored him, He did not saddle him with guilt nor debt for the time He spent with him. He wanted Peter to do God's work because he loved Him. Is it ever appropriate to work for God with respect to how He has or will bless us? Gratitude is a legitimate motivation for serving God and should be common among believers. The greatest gift (sacrifice) one can give God, however, is the gift (sacrifice) of love.

And now abideth faith, hope, charity, these
three; but the greatest of these is charity.
1 Corinthians 13:13

Love is the foundation of the gospel message. The entire thirteenth chapter of Corinthians is devoted to the subject. In it, we find that everything done without love is for naught. We can have faith that moves mountains or hope that sustains our commitment to endure until the end, but nothing will achieve God's favor like love.

God's plan of salvation was not developed so we could speak in tongues, though the gift of tongues were given in the book of Acts. His plan was not developed so we could prophesy to one another. His plan was not devised so we could be healed and walk in prosperity, although we thank God for these displays of grace and mercy. The grand design of salvation's plan aims to provide an unparalleled opportunity to receive, experience, and share God's love. The greatest thing we can do for God is reciprocate the love He demonstrates towards us and love Him unconditionally.

Chapter 4

FRIENDSHIP AND
FELLOWSHIP
FACILITATED

A friend loveth at all times, and a brother is
born for adversity.
Proverbs 17:17

We typically enjoy spending time with the
people we call our friends. These are the people we
depend on for consolation, good council, and a
listening ear. We have confidence in them when we
cannot rely on anyone else. Regardless of the
situation, they are here for us. A true friend will
overcome petty disputes to help us when we fall.
They look past their feelings and preferences and can
always be found in our corner when we need them
most.

The greatest compliment is to be called a friend. My wife, whom I love dearly, seemed overwhelmed the first time I told her that she was my best friend. She understood the statement to mean that I not only loved her, but also saw her as trustworthy and faithful. It implied that I would always search for her first when I needed assistance with a problem or a difficult decision. She would be the first person contacted if I received news worth celebrating. If considering her a friend meant so much, how much more significant is it to be called a friend of God?

> And the scripture was fulfilled which saith,
> Abraham believed God, and it was imputed
> unto him for righteousness: and he was called
> the Friend of God.
> James 2:23

It is one thing to know God as a friend to mankind, but it is a completely different thing to be considered a personal friend of God. God shows genuine concern for humanity and fulfills every characteristic of a friend. We are told in Genesis 3:8 that He visited Adam in the cool of the day. This was a time and place of fellowship. After man sinned, God issued punishments – sin is a work of the flesh, and a just God will not allow work to be done without compensating the worker with due wages. The Bible does not say whether He was angry with man or not. It does imply that the incident was not deplorable enough to end His friendship with Adam.

Angry or not, verse 21 states that He made "coats of skins, and clothed them," because He knew the leaves they fashioned would not endure nor would they protect them from the elements of a raging planet. This is what friends do. They look beyond the broken relationship and assists in the wellbeing and prosperity of those dear to them.

Abram, being called a friend of God, found a special place in His heart. How did he get there? He believed God. From the time God called him out of Haran, he remained faithful. He proved himself a friend of God by dropping his personal agendas and pursued the prosperity of His will and plan. Abram may have had other friends at the time, but he chose his God above all else. In doing so, he proved his love and friendship thus becoming our example and the father of the faithful.

A man that hath friends must show himself
friendly: and there is a friend that sticketh
closer than a brother.
Proverbs 18:24

Being a friend brings with it undeniable responsibility. A friend will offend from time to time, but they will never forsake you – even in the toughest of times. Therefore, being a friend can be extremely taxing; we can only emotionally, spiritually, and physically assist a limited number of people at any given time.

God, on the other hand, is omnipotent and omnipresent. He is all-powerful and in all places. Therefore, he can accommodate an infinite number of needy people – as all of us are to varying degrees.

Proverbs 18:24 has long been one of my favorite Bible verses. For years, I understand the verse to mean that people who want friends must first show themselves to be a friend. Looking at the scripture now, I see the taxing nature of friendship. The scripture in the Amplified Bible reads, "The man of too many friends will be broken in pieces and come to ruin." The more friends we have, the more complex life becomes.

Friends are demanding, require a lot of attention, expect special privileges, and assume to have unlimited access to you. Limiting the number of friends we have at any given time helps us manage the demands of friendship. God, in contrast, is a reliable friend in all instances. He is a friend as familiar as family. Salvation ask whether we are willing to show ourselves friendly to Him.

> And let them make me a sanctuary; that I may
> dwell among them.
> Exodus 25:8

Does absence makes the heart grow fonder? Perhaps. Fellowship is an inherent part of friendship. The absence of uninhibited fellowship fuels the fires of hope (that longs for a reunion) and love (that focuses on the good and looks past the undesirable traits of the beloved). Fellowship from a distance can also be difficult, painful, and unsustainable. Long-distance relationships require a special commitment. Love must be nurtured in order for it to endure the discomforts of separation. Working to close the physical gap and preparing for a restoration of intimacy are vitally important.

The plan of salvation exemplifies God's desire to restore the intimate fellowship lost after Adam sinned; but before God could implement the New Testament phase of His salvation plan, He used a tabernacle. God gave Moses specific instructions on how to build the tabernacle, a place designed specifically to facilitate intimate fellowship with Him. The tabernacle consisted of the Holy and Most Holy Places and was surrounded by a fenced-in courtyard.

The Tabernacle's design is a blueprint for perfect fellowship with God. All who desired fellowshipped with God were required to enter the same way, provide a sacrifice, be cleansed, enter the Holy Place to worship, and then enter the manifested presence of God in the Holy of Hollies. Let's take a closer look...

THE COURTYARD

The Fine Linen Fence

> And thou shalt make a courtyard for the
> tabernacle: for the south side southward there
> shall be hangings for the court of fine twined
> linen of an hundred cubits long for one side:
> Exodus 27:9

The courtyard, a transition place between the natural and the spiritual, was enclosed by a fine linen fence. The word used for linen here is "shaysh" (Strong's 8336) whose root means to "bleach or whiten." The fine linen fence was a symbol of righteousness as noted by its white color (Revelation 19:8). It was seven and a half feet high and supported by pillars about seven and a half feet apart. The height prevented spectators from looking over the fence. Only those who entered in through the gate could fellowship with God in His Tabernacle.

Entry into the courtyard was the first step in proper fellowship with God. God ordered a single entry point to the courtyard. This ensured everyone who entered the courtyard entered from the east (Numbers 3:38) to worship towards the west perhaps in contrast to their Egyptian counterparts who worshiped the sun, which rises in the east. Entering the courtyard in this direction, facing west, symbolized repentance or the turning away from the world. To enter into fellowship with God, we must be willing to turn our affections towards Him, in the opposite direction of the world.

The single gate also required submission to God's will and way. Isaiah 55:7 says, "Let the wicked forsake his way, and the unrighteous man his thoughts: and let him return unto the LORD, and He will have mercy upon him; and to our God, for He will abundantly pardon." The courtyard's entry point dictated worship in a manner chosen by God.

The gate to the Tabernacle is similar in significance to the door to sheepfold as described by Jesus (John 10:1). God always sets the requisite terms to enter a covenant fellowship with Him. All who worshiped Him in the Tabernacle were required to do so by entering in at the gate. In John 10:7-9, Jesus said that He is the door to the sheepfold, which makes Him the only option for salvation. Anyone who enters in (to fellowship with God) must do so according to His design. They must do so through Jesus who is the way, truth, and life (John 14:6).

The Bronze Altar

> And thou shalt make an altar of shittim wood,
> five cubits long, and five cubits broad; the
> altar shall be foursquare: and the height
> thereof shall be three cubits.
> Exodus 27:1

Providing an acceptable sacrifice is the second step in experiencing proper fellowship with God. Just inside the entrance was a bronze altar, which worshipers used to present a sacrifice to God. The bronze altar was a place where sinners could atone for their sins through a blood sacrifice, facilitating free worship.

The altar was made of wood, overlaid with brass (Exodus 27:2). The wood provided a strong and structurally sound altar; however, wood cannot resist the consuming power of the altar's fire. The overlay of brass protected the altar from the flames. Like the wood, the children of Israel were strong-willed and often strayed from the will of God. The brass overlay symbolizes the grace and mercy of God that covers and protects the believer from the consuming fire of his wrath.

The altar was a square box, five cubits (about seven and a half feet) long and five cubits wide. The altar of sacrifice was an equal-sided structure constructed as a means to stay God's judgment. The equal sides demonstrated the accuracy, precision, and impartiality of God's judgment. His judgment is balanced, consistent, and righteous. All who exercise faith can experience His favor.

The altar was three cubits (four and a half feet) high, which elevated the top of the altar requiring the sacrifice to be lifted. Hence, sacrifices were "offered up" to God, and the blood ran down. Making sacrifices in this way demonstrates that we are not equal but subordinate to God in power, righteousness, authority...in every way. When Jesus said in John 12:32, "And if I, be lifted up from the earth, will draw all men unto me," He not only pointed to His impending sacrifice for the propitiation – the appeasement – of human sin but also provided a clear demonstration of His (and mankind's) inherent subordination to God.

A lamb was sacrificed as a burnt offering upon the altar every morning and evening (Exodus 29:38-42), one lamb as the first act of the day and the second lamb as the last. Both sacrifices were accompanied by a meat (bread) and drink (wine) offering, which bears a striking resemblance to the meat and drink offering prior to the crucifixion of Jesus. Jesus took bread and wine from the dinner table and said they represented His body (God's word) and His blood (God's redemption), respectively. The work Christ did on the cross eliminated the need for physical sacrifices, but the value of the daily activity seen in Exodus 29 remains.

Pausing every morning and evening to fellowship with God is an essential act that focuses and binds the activities of our day, sheltering us within God's purpose and plan. Believers should make it a priority to begin and end each day with a bread (word of God) and wine (prayer to God) offering. Beginning the day with the word of God and prayer regulates our minds and sharpens the weapons of our warfare before the enemy unveils his plans to kill, steal, and destroy (John 10:10). Ending the day with the word and prayer gives us an opportunity to reflect on the good and bad decisions of the day and chart tomorrow's path to a more abundant life.

The Bronze Laver

> Thou shalt also make a laver of brass, and his
> foot also of brass, to wash withal: and thou
> shalt put it between the tabernacle of the
> congregation and the altar, and thou shalt put
> water therein.
> Exodus 30:18

Between the altar of sacrifice and the Tabernacle of worship stood the bronze laver. Exodus 38:8 states that Moses "made the laver of brass...of the mirrors of the ministering women..." All who entered in through the gate, offered up a sacrifice and paused to wash their hands and feet would encounter a reflection of themselves in the Bronze Laver. The reflection in the Bronze Laver invited a moment of self-examination, which leads to spiritual clarity. Self-examination is the third step in proper fellowship with God.

Very few can pass a mirror without stealing a glance at themselves. On an average day, we see other people more than we see ourselves. Perhaps this is one of the reasons we are more familiar with the strengths and weaknesses of others than we are with our own. Notwithstanding, there are moments when we are forced to pause in front of a mirror and comb our hair, brush our teeth, shave our beard, or apply makeup. In these moments of self-examination, we are reminded of our flaws and uncover things about ourselves once overlooked.

In 1 Corinthians 11:28, Paul said, "let a man examine himself, and so let him eat of that bread, and drink of that cup." This was a key phrase used to communicate the importance of self-examination prior to having fellowship with other believers in the last ordinance left by Christ, Holy Communion (also known as the "Last Supper" or "Lord's Supper"). Holy Communion is a worship experience where believers show gratitude for the saving sacrifice of the Son of God. Paul, in verse 28, encouraged the church at Corinth to gaze into a symbolic mirror and perform an honest, personal examination prior to engaging in fellowship with God in the backdrop of humble appreciation of the death, burial, and resurrection of Jesus Christ.

As it stands, a proper view of God is preceded by a proper view of one's self. Seeing ourselves as we truly are, in the context of worship, reminds us how flawed we are compared to God's perfection, how unrighteous we are compared to God's righteousness, and how unclean we are compared to

God's holiness. Those who looked into the Bronze Laver were met with a proper view of themselves, but the climax of the experience came when their portrait was broken as they dipped their hands into the water to cleanse their hands and feet.

The washing process disturbed the water and, consequently, the image within the Bronze Laver. Herein is the power of God to wash away our sins and dismantle our flaws. As the self-image became indiscernible during the washing process, the cleansing power of God cancels the guilt and shame that comes with seeing ourselves as we really are. God's cleansing power transforms our flawed character, unrighteous path, and unclean hands. It prepares us to enter into the Tabernacle of worship with holy hands lifted unto the Lord in the beauty of uninhibited fellowship.

THE TABERNACLE

And let them make me a sanctuary; that I may
dwell among them. According to all that I
shew thee, after the pattern of the tabernacle,
and the pattern of all the instruments thereof,
even so shall ye make it.
Exodus 25:8-9

The Holy Place

The Holy Place resided inside the Tabernacle. It was set aside as a sanctuary separated from sinful nature and acts of mankind. It provided a sense of heaven on earth, a place where God dwelled with man on His terms. Those who fellowshipped with Him entered in from a single direction through the fine linen fence, provided a sacrifice on the brazen altar, and washed in the bronze laver. These rites of consecration were necessary measures to enter the Holy Place, as the priests did daily.

The Table of Shewbread

And thou shalt set upon the table shewbread
before me alway.
Exodus 25:30

Upon entering the Holy Place, the table of shewbread, made of acacia wood and overlaid with gold, was positioned to the right as facing the Holy of Holies. Twelve loaves of bread were ordered to occupy the table at all times. The twelve loaves, undoubtedly, represented the twelve tribes of Israel. The fact that these loaves were ever present before the Lord points to the everlasting covenant God made with Abram. As the shewbread was always present, the covenant relationship with Abram would endure from one generation to the next.

The bread was to abide from Sabbath to Sabbath and could only be eaten by the priests. The priests must have baked the bread on the day prior to the Sabbath – the Mosaic Law mandated that the Sabbath be a day of rest. From this, we infer that the priest entered the Holy Place prepared for worship.

Preparation should always precede praise. If a fresh batch of bread was placed before the Lord at the dawning of every Sabbath, then it naturally follows that our praise should be fresh and new. If God does a new thing in us and if His mercies and compassions are new every morning (Lamentations 3:23), is it not a reasonable expectation for us to "sing a new song" unto the Lord (Isaiah 42:10)? Our new song is a function of the heart not lyrics or melodies. The priest used the same recipe, but the bread was new every week.

Bread is also a symbol of God's provision. God instructed Israel, the night of the Passover in Egypt, to eat unleavened bread as He worked out the provisions of their deliverance (Exodus 12:20). God provided manna (bread) from heaven when the Israelites were in wilderness surviving as refugees from Egypt (Exodus 16:49). Jesus used bread to symbolize His body, which is eternally provided as a sacrifice for our sins (Mark 14:22). The ever-present bread points to God's inexhaustible provision. The expiration of the shewbread makes clear that the blessings of God are for a season, but He has infinite resources to supply.

The Altar of Incense

> And thou shalt make an altar to burn incense
> upon: of shittim wood shalt thou make it.
> Exodus 30:1-2

The burning of incense unto to the Lord was also among the priest's daily activities, and we also learn by reading Luke 1:8-9 that the burning of the incense characterized a time of prayer and fellowship with God. This was a special time indeed. So much so that all incense offered had to comply with God's prescription as described in Exodus 30:34.

The incense was to be kindled twice a day so it could burn all day. So should prayer be in the life of a Christian who enters the Holy Place and communes with God. We should find ourselves in a perpetual state of prayer. We no longer need a priest to burn incense for us. Hebrews 4:16 tells us that we can now come "boldly unto the throne of grace, that we may obtain mercy."

In our boldness, however, maintaining the sanctity of the altar of incense is vital. The use of this altar for any purpose other than burning incense prescribed by God was strictly forbidden. All other incense were considered strange fire, and the altar that bore them could not double as a sacrificial nor offertory altar (v. 9). It was sanctified for fellowship and nothing else.

When we, through prayer, draw nigh to God, we do so with genuine sincerity. Prayer and sacrifice are complimentary acts of fellowship. However, we should never consider prayer a sacrifice. Prayer is a time when believers, the children of the most-high

God, pause to have fellowship with the creator because we love Him and desire to focus on His priorities. Paul said it best in the eight chapter of his letter to the Romans. He said we are adopted, and thereby "we cry, Abba, Father," a term used only by family members in reference to their father. Loosely translated, we call Him "Daddy."

As for the strange fire, who can formulate an incense that releases a more excellent aroma than those devised by God? If we go to a restaurant and ask for a steak, we expect to receive a steak when the waiter returns with the main course. We would be disappointed, perhaps offended, if chicken was served instead. Whether we like chicken or not would not be the issue. Most of us would simply want what we asked for and would not settle for what the cook felt like preparing, especially if we were expected to pay the bill.

John 9 speaks of a man blind from birth who meets Jesus and receives a complete restoration of his sight. After deliberating and debating with the Pharisees (Jews who maintained a strict observance of traditions and the Mosaic Law) over the character of Christ, the man concluded in verse 31 that "God heareth not sinners: but if any man be a worshiper of God, and doeth His will, him He heareth." He was convinced that, if he being blind from birth could now see, Christ must have been sent from God. Jesus was not only sent from God, but God also hears his prayer. The man's words are now a source of debate for those who ask, "Does God hear a sinner's prayer?"

Whether God hears a sinner's prayer is a question for the ages, but one thing is sure: Jesus is the only way to the Father and no one can get to the Father except through Him (John 14:6). Attempting to get to the Father any other way is unacceptable; it is strange fire. Strange fire, like chicken served instead of the steak, contradicts God's formula for prayer, worship, and communion.

When incense were burned in the Holy Place, the smoke and smell infiltrated the Holy of Holies and went before the Lord. Jesus is the incense that God ordered and prepared. He goes before us into the Holy of Holies and stands in our stead. The beauty of His holiness overshadows the stench of our sin, and Holy Communion is made possible.

The Holy of Holies

In this section, we focus on what the Bible calls the Most Holy Place; most commonly referred to as the Holy of Holies. The outer and inner courts were places where man came to meet God. The Holy of Holies is the place where God came to meet man. Unlike the Holy Place where priest entered daily, they only crossed the threshold of the Holy of Holies once per year. Furthermore, only a select few were allowed to go beyond the veil.

The Veil

> And thou shalt hang up the veil under the taches, that thou mayest bring in thither within the veil the ark of the testimony: and the veil shall divide unto you between the holy place and the most holy.
> Exodus 26:33

The veil was designed to be a separator between the common and the most holy. God set aside the sons of Levi and laid upon them the privilege (or burden) of going behind the veil to make atonement for the sins of Israel once per year. This was serious business, a duty reserved only for the high priest. The price for not strictly following God's instructions was death. The holiness of God is a purifying fire, and the frailty of man cannot survive its consuming power.

Moses' interaction with the Israelites after his experience on Mount Sinai brings this idea into focus. In Exodus 33:18-23, Moses requested to see God's glory, and He fulfilled his desire by allowing Moses to catch a glimpse of His backside as He passed by him. God refused to show him His face. It is probable that Moses would not have (physically or mentally) comprehended God's eternal glory upon seeing Him face to face. Surely, death or insanity would have been the result.

After only seeing God's back, the Bible says that Moses had to wear a veil when he spoke to the people because the glory of his face was more than they could bear. The veil allowed that which was common to communicate with that which was touched by the glory of God. Moses wore the veil among the people and removed it when he spoke to God. This act of removing the veil when speaking to God was later accomplished once and for all through the sacrificial work of Christ.

And, behold, the veil of the temple was rent in
twain from the top to the bottom; and the earth
did quake, and the rocks rent;
Matthew 27: 51

At the utterance of three words, "It is finished," Jesus bridged the gap between God and humanity. It was at the sounding of those three words that the veil in the temple was torn from top to bottom. The completion of His sacrifice ensured His place as the eternal High Priest, culminating the longstanding duty of the high priests that came before.

The tearing of the veil exposed the glory of God to all who are willing to enter and be cleansed by the blood of Jesus (1 John 1:17). The high priests were not allowed to enter the Holy of Holies without the blood of a sacrifice. The sacrificial blood was their rite of passage into the presence of God. Jesus, being the perfect sacrifice, brought about a perfect atonement, and His blood has become our rite of passage.

The high priest made atonement for the sins of the people as well as his own. Jesus' ability to live in this world without personal sin made His sacrifice and act of atonement perfect. His completely selfless act of love makes it possible for Him to vouch for all who desire to have a close relationship with Jehovah.

Like Moses, the high priests who entered the presence of God had to do so alone, and the veil could not stand between them. Corporate worship and prayer, in the congregation of the righteous or with two or three believers, is encouraged. In fact, He inhabits the praises of His people (Psalms 22:3). Entering the Holy of Holies, however, must be done alone. He desires fellowship with you and you alone.

When Moses received God's plan for Israel and the Ten Commandments, he was alone. When Jesus talked to God in the garden and the disciples witnessed His glory, He was alone. When Jesus died on the cross and entered the Holy of Holies, He was alone. All who name the name of Christ are now a royal priesthood, a holy nation, a peculiar people and a chosen generation (1 Peter 2:9) and are granted access to the Holy of Holies, but we must always enter alone.

The Ark of the Testimony

> And thou shalt put into the ark the testimony
> which I shall give thee.
> Exodus 25:16

The ark of the testimony was kept behind the veil. Originally, only one thing was housed in the ark of the testimony, the Ten Commandments. Later, two things were added, manna (the bread that fell from heaven while Israel was in the wilderness) and Aaron's budding rod. As with the shewbread, the items maintained in the ark of the testimony exemplifies God's provision for His people.

The Ten Commandments represented His first provision, His word. It takes faith to believe that He is behind the vail, but it takes action to enter in and experience what awaits. Once in His presence, He speaks to us concerning His will, and the scriptures that are unclear become intelligible. Some disagree with the notion that God speaks to us, but their disbelief serves as evidence to the fact that they have not been in His presence. Those who enter His presence and experience His word are filled with His glory and changed forever.

The manna represents His second provision, His resources. When God began raining manna from heaven, He continued to do so throughout Israel's 40-year journey in the wilderness (Exodus 16:35). The manna kept in the ark was a reminder that God meets the needs of His people, thus worrying about the needs and activities of tomorrow is a pointless endeavor.

When we enter the presence of God, the cares and necessities of tomorrow become insignificant. We realize that God knows all of our needs, and He will never fail to provide for them. We choose to believe in every instance that God will not allow us to die of hunger in the wilderness when He has unlimited resources. We become resourceful because He is full of resources.

Aaron's budding rod represents the third provision, God's protection in His purpose (Numbers 17). After being stranded in the wilderness for an extended period of time, several of the sons of Levi began a revolt against Moses and Aaron. Their objective was to elevate themselves to Aaron's position. Their selfish ambition only served to bring them to destruction at the hand of God.

What does this have to do with Aaron's budding rod? Everything! God directed each tribe of Israel to choose a representative. Aaron was chosen by God to represent the house of Levi. The rods of the representatives were brought before the Lord, and the next day only Aaron's rod was filled with buds, blossoms, and almonds.

Aaron's budding rod was a clear indication of God's approval of his position as the high priest and His protection against those who would attempt to overthrow him in his purpose. God's calling is sure. When we are in His presence, He assures us through miracles seen and unseen that He called us for a purpose and will protect us in the execution of that purpose. In His presence, we find confidence in the discovery of who we are and what we are destined to do and become.

The Cherubim

> And thou shalt make two cherubims of gold, of beaten work shall thou make them, in the two ends of the mercy seat.
> Exodus 25:18

I wrestled with the significance of the cherubim for some time. I was convinced that the cherubim symbolized an aspect of salvation, but what their presence meant, as it relates to communion with Him, was the question. I spoke to several ministers about it. All had insight but none had considered the question before and had to admit that they too were unsure.

The most agreeable answer came via e-mail from the minister that inspired me to write this book, Elder Cedric Lang. His solution was found in the number two; there were two cherubim. Further examination and prayer revealed the perfect symbolism of the cherubim.

The minimum number needed for a covenant or agreement is two. This is also the number of balance. The cherubim must have symbolized a balanced covenant between God and man, but what else could they have represented? Perfection. The cherubim in their perfection shadowed God's desire to have a *perfectly balanced* relationship with mankind.

Like the cherubim made of gold, God places a high value on his relationship with mankind. Moreover, a perfectly balanced relationship doesn't just happen. It is a "beaten work" that takes time and effort.

Isaiah 53:5 says, "[Jesus] was wounded for our transgressions, he was bruised for our iniquities: the chastisement of our peace was upon him; and with his stripes we are healed." The first half of our relationship was forged through the blood of Jesus. The second half is hammered into existence through persistent yet precise trials and tribulations, which push us toward God; prayer, which familiarizes us with God; and forgiveness, which makes us acceptable to God.

God wants to hear our every desire, and He wants us to listen to His every word. As the wings of the cherubim touched, we must also allow the word of God to touch our hearts through daily prayer and meditation.

The Mercy Seat

> And there I will meet with thee, and I will
> commune with the from above the mercy seat,
> from between the two cherubim which are
> upon the ark of the testimony, of all things
> which I will give thee in commandment unto
> the children of Israel.
> Exodus 25:22

The mercy seat was located in a pivotal place between God and the priests. Its mere placement speaks volumes. Consider the above scripture. We see four positional words that emphasize God's position in relation to the mercy seat: with, above, between, and upon.

God said He would meet *with* the priest behind the vail. A meeting cannot take place unless there are at least two parties. God never fails to show up, but how often are we absent or neglect to meet with Him? Nevertheless, He is faithful and invites us behind the veil to obtain mercy and fulfill His objective to commune with us at the mercy seat.

Moreover, He said He would commune with the priest *above* the mercy seat. Note that God did not sit on the mercy seat; He sat above it. This posture, sitting above the mercy seat, facilitated an undisturbed view of the mercy seat, which was *between* the two cherubim. The message in the between suggests that communion, or perfect balance between God and humanity, hinges on God's mercy.

Before God can consider a relationship with us, He has to first consider His mercy. Without mercy, a balanced relationship with God is not possible. Mankind has nothing to offer in a relationship with God that is of significant or equal value. God's mercy, for the sake of divine fellowship, grants us the privilege of trading a penny for a dollar, an example that falls far short of the true value of His mercy.

Finally, the seat of mercy was positioned *upon* the ark of the testimony, between God and His word. In order for God to acknowledge His commandments or promises, He had to first consider mercy. The sins of mankind inhibited communion with God because they were a consistent offense to His commandments. The mercy seat stood as a spiritual buffer between God and His word. Without it, God's word condemns man, and His promises become void for lack of a suitable recipient. God's desire is communion not condemnation; condemnation can never yield a loving fellowship.

God's mercy holds our fellowship together. It grants access to the Most Holy One. It balances the scales of our relationship. It shields us from the condemnation of His word and facilitates the fulfilment of His promises. God's mercy is essential.

The Something Missing

> And there shall be no night there; and they
> need no candle, neither light of the sun; for the
> Lord God giveth them light...
> Revelation 22: 5

In Exodus 25, God ordered three things to be placed in the Most Holy Place. However, if we look closer, we see a fourth. As we have discussed, the three things God ordered the priest to put in the Most Holy Place were the ark of the testimony, the mercy seat, and the cherubim. The fourth is not readily apparent. Actually, it can't be seen at all.

The fourth was darkness. The lamp, tended to by Aaron and his sons, was placed on the opposite side of the vail, in the Holy Place. This could not have been accidental. God was the only light allowed behind the vail; He is the perfect light. He is the one and only God, the light of the world, and He does not share His glory with another.

All other light is artificial. Light is produced through the consumption, interaction, or manipulation of natural occurring elements. Natural light sources are extinguishable, limited in radiance, and a finite source of illumination. They cannot compare to the light we receive from God. His light cannot be compromised. It overshadows the glory of all others.

Furthermore, everything behind the veil was either overlaid or made with gold, indicating that the place of worship, i.e. the time we spend with God, should be considered valuable. Matthew 6:21 records Jesus saying, "where your treasure is, there will your heart be also." If we treasure spending time with God, our hearts will anticipate entering the Most Holy Place knowing that the presence of God awaits us.

THE ATONEMENT

> But the goat, on which the lot fell to be the
> scapegoat, shall be presented alive before the
> Lord, to make an atonement with him, and to
> let him go for a scapegoat into the wilderness.
> Leviticus 16:10

Annually, on the Day of Atonement, the high priest made a sacrifice of a lamb and sprinkled its blood on the mercy seat (Hebrews 9:25). Only the priests were allowed to enter the Holy of Holies during the time of atonement. Today, because of the work of Christ, we are neither required to go to a physical temple nor enter a special room. Christ has become our high priest and has opened the Holy of Holies to every person who looks to Him for salvation.

Again, God's purpose for the tabernacle was fellowship, and His love-driven desire for fellowship could not be satisfied with a relationship that was limited to once per year. He planned to change this one-man-once-a-year fellowship to an every-person-every-day fellowship. The price would be high, but "no greater love hath no man than this that He would lay down his life for a friend" (John 15:13).

On the Day of Atonement, the high priests were expected to procure two goats: one as a sacrifice for the remission of sin and the other a scapegoat. The priests were commanded to cast lots to decide which goat would be the sacrifice and which would be the scapegoat. Perhaps choosing the appropriate sacrifice in this manner left the decision in the hands of God. After the first goat was sacrificed, the priests were commanded to place both hands on the head of the second and confess the iniquities of the children of Israel. Afterward, bearing the sins of Israel, the goat was released into the wilderness.

By becoming the sacrifice and the scapegoat, Christ followed this method of atonement. Those who are students of the word know that He was the perfect sacrifice. In the fifth chapter of Revelation, John saw a vision of Him as the Lion of Judah, the Root of David, and the Lamb as it had been slain.

When John the Baptist saw Jesus in Bethabara, he said, "Behold the Lamb of God, which taketh away the sin of the world" (John 1:29). John, with his proclamation, associated Jesus with the purpose of the second goat. Not only was He destined to be the sacrifice for sin; but He was also chosen to be the scapegoat, released to take the sin away.

Furthermore, John displayed his complete understanding of God's plan to refurbish our relationship with Him. His plan extended beyond fellowship with the children of Israel. Jesus came to be the scapegoat for the world. The death of Christ marked the end of an era where only a chosen few were privileged to enjoy intimate fellowship with God.

In Remembrance of Me

For as often as ye eat this bread, and drink this cup, ye do show the Lord's death till he come.
1 Corinthians 11: 26

Jesus displayed His unity with the Father in the idea of fellowship. God ordered a sanctuary to be built in the Old Testament. We became His sanctuaries at the tearing of the vail, which signified the beginning of a greater testament. Jesus, with a new covenant, emphasized fellowship through Holy Communion.

116

The disciples would often break bread together. Christians today rarely get together without including some sort of food item(s). Food and fellowship go hand-in-hand. Therefore, the last supper Christ shared with His disciples held great significance.

The disciples, per Jewish custom, were very particular about with whom they ate. Eating with someone served as a sign of mutual agreement or acceptance. Knowing this, we better understand why Jesus asked the disciples to share communion and to "...do this in remembrance of me" (Luke 22:19, AMP). These words were spoken after He gave the disciples bread and again after He gave them wine.

The bread represented His body that was pierced by nails, whips, thorns, and a spear, and the wine represented the blood that seeped from His open wounds. Jesus charges us to remember His sacrifice for it atones for our sins and sets us free from condemnation. Eating with Him from generation to generation is a perpetual reminder that we are forgiven and free from guilt.

David said God prepared a table before him in the presence of his enemies (Psalms 23). David understood that God could give him the power and a heart to forgive his enemies, including those he respected (Saul) and those who rose from his own bosom (Absalom). In the same manner, Jesus was able to eat with His betrayer the night before His arrest and crucifixion, which worked for our glory.

Communion reminds us that we are accepted and forgiven. It gives us the opportunity to accept and forgive those who have offended us and restores a peaceful relationship among our spiritual brothers and sisters. Like the parent who agonizes when siblings fight, God desires that we, his family, eat together as an expression of love and friendship. He left Holy Communion to help make us one, even as He and the Father are one (John 17:22).

Chapter 5

THE TEMPLE OF GOD

And I saw no temple therein: for the Lord God
Almighty and the Lamb were the temple of it.
Revelation 21:22

Most of the time, all we need is an idea, and
our imagination becomes our only limitation. Once
an idea is born, it grows at the rate of our ability to
dream. Dreaming is not a physically demanding
activity, but making our dreams a reality is rarely
easy. Untimely and unforeseen challenges inevitably
aggravate our carefully calculated plans.

The major difficulty of any task lies with our
dependence on others to complete it. Project
managers are regularly driven to renegotiate terms,
change deadlines, apply temporary fixes, and
develop creative measures to keep the plan on track,
on cost, and on schedule.

Creation, from Genesis to Revelation, is God's ultimate project. Adam and Eve introduced a complication for Him by introducing sin. Therefore, He had to make adjustments to ensure His dream of perfect fellowship with mankind was realized. One of the temporary fixes He created was a temple.

When God created the heavens and the earth, both were perfect and perfectly suited for flawless fellowship with God. Thus, a temple was not necessary in the Garden of Eden. However, when Adam sinned, sin brought with it the corruption of a once holy planet and the need to consecrate a new place for worship.

God is sovereign, thus, His creations are sufficient at completion. The fact that He didn't place a temple in the Garden of Eden for Adam and Eve to worship suggests that the Garden was sufficiently equipped for worship and communion with God. Sin brought about the need for a temple, a need that will expire in Heaven when God becomes our Temple (Revelation 21:22). Heaven will bring to fruition the promise of God's eternal presence.

The fact that a temple wasn't necessary in the beginning of time nor will it be in the end of time begs the question: What is its significance between the Garden of Eden and New Jerusalem?

A NOBLE THOUGHT

Construct Godly Dreams

> And it came to pass, when the king sat in his house, and the LORD had given him rest round about from all his enemies; That the king said unto Nathan the prophet, See now, I dwell in an house of cedar, but the ark of God dwelleth within curtains.
> 2 Samuel 7:1-2

All things that are planned, designed, or created must first begin with a thought or inspiration. Inevitably, the person who dreams of dramatic change is rarely the person that engineers it to completion. Martin Luther King dreamed of freedom and equality but did not live to see it accomplished. Albert Einstein dreamed of space travel but went to his grave before the first space craft entered Earth's orbit. Isaiah dreamed of the Messiah but did not live to see his Deliverer. In this chapter, we examine David, the King of Israel, who dared to dream beyond his years.

121

David dreamed of a house for the Ark of the Covenant. According to 2 Samuel 7:1-2, three things were the catalyst for his inspiration. They are also key building blocks for seizing the opportunity to do a work for God.

First, David's dream came as he "sat in his house." He was at home, the most comfortable place on earth – at least it should be. It's a place of safety and freedom. As a child growing up in Houston, my mother insisted, "Cedrick, be in this house before the sun goes down!" According to her philosophy, most mischief took place at night, and being safe meant being home before nightfall.

David found rest "in his house." Some go to clubs, bars, gyms, sporting events, etc. to deal with stress and relax. However, if they can't find rest in their house, there is a good chance they will not find it anywhere. We cannot experience true freedom until we have experienced the freedom of being ourselves without the burden of human expectation. David's house was the only place he could feel free to be David. Everywhere else, he had to be King David or David the great warrior.

Like David, we can better focus on who God is and how to properly honor Him when we withdraw to a place where we aren't preoccupied with appropriate appearances and responses. David had to first minimize his concern with everything else in his life before he could begin to dream of building God's temple.

Second, we notice that the "Lord had given him rest round about from all his enemies" (2 Samuel 7:1). Life is full of trouble, and times of rest are often few and far between. What is that ole saying? "If it's not one thing, it's another." How we manage the fleeting moments between the one thing and another will seed the next cycle of ups and downs, gains and losses, masteries and missteps, and successes and failures.

David did not spend his idle time considering how he could get ahead. He did not expend his days looking back on the glorious battles he'd won. He was a man of war, but he did not spend his days contemplating ways to improve his army's effectiveness. David used this break in warfare to think about what he could do for the God who consistently brought him victory.

Third, David took note of his possessions and realized that they spoke volumes concerning his heart. He took inventory of his way of life and compared it to that of the God who provided him with the wealth he enjoyed. David thought it a great insult for his own house to be made of fine wood and the place set aside for God to be enclosed in curtains. No doubt, God was his true treasure.

David's love for God ran deep and was demonstrated in his gratitude; David's gratitude changed his perception of his wealth. We, the chosen people of God, receive blessings from Him and boast of His goodness, but how often do these blessings cause us to consider how the prosperity of God's work compare to our personal prosperity? Our professed love for God would do well to display the type of gratitude expressed by David.

David understood that doing a work for God was going to take a sacrifice of resources. He used this time of rest from his enemies to realign the sight of his heart with the things of God. All believers should be so wise.

The Contradiction of War

> But God said unto me, Thou shalt not build a
> house for my name, because thou hast been a
> man of war, and hast shed blood.
> 1 Chronicles 28:3

David stands among the great heroes of the Bible. He proved himself to be a man of loyalty in refusing to take part in assassinating Saul (1 Samuel 24:1-7, 26:1-13), the king of Israel who wanted him dead (1 Samuel 19:1-2). He was a man of great faith, proven in his statement to a giant named Goliath.

> Then said David to the Philistine, Thou comest
> to me with a sword, and with a spear, and with
> a shield: but I come to thee in the name of the
> LORD of hosts, …This day will the LORD
> deliver thee into mine hand…that all the earth
> may know that there is a God in Israel.
> 1 Samuel 17:45-46

He was a God-led leader, proven in his prayer for direction.

> Therefore David inquired of the LORD,
> saying, Shall I go and smite these Philistines?
> And the LORD said unto David, Go, and smite
> the Philistines and save Keiliah.
> 1 Samuel 23:2

David, in all his greatness and favor with God and the children of Israel, was denied the opportunity to fulfill his greatest dream. God refused David's request to build a temple (1 Chronicles 28:3). The reason seems worse than the answer. It is bad enough that he wasn't able to build a temple for the God he loved and faithfully served, but he could not build the temple because he was obedient to the God he faithfully served.

David was a dreamer, but his role was to be a warrior for the children of Israel. During his reign as king, the children of Israel needed a general to lead them to victory over enemies who were determined to subdue them. The plans of a king with the mind of an architect, during this period of unrest, would have been in constant jeopardy of being thwarted.

This is the contradiction of war. Progress for David depended on both growth and development; growth came through war and development though construction. Warring and building, when accomplished simultaneously, become competing activities where one suffers at the expense of the other.

The early church faced the contradiction of war and construction. The disciples, in the book of Acts, spent much of their time warring against the spiritual and political leaders of their day. They traveled from city to city and temple to temple disputing with the elders concerning the nature and divinity of Christ. The spiritual leaders opposed them for disrupting their authority. The political leaders tossed them in prison for disrupting their economic and civil strongholds.

The disciples understood, however, that they needed help. It was not possible for them to simultaneously contend with the Pharisees, Sadducees, and Potentates while developing the new coverts won in spiritual battle. Some remained in Jerusalem, and others were dispatched two by two. Paul was a spiritual warrior for Christ, but when he landed in prison, he took advantage of his situation. He transformed his cell into a place of rest where he could build on the faith of believers through letters of instruction and reproof.

This is a lesson worth learning. Matthew 5:25 says, "Agree with thine adversary quickly." The point of this scripture is geared toward the avoidance of legislation – avoiding the legal system is generally a good idea. Trials can last for weeks, months, or years. People in legal battles are forced to put their dreams and aspirations on hold until the situation is resolved.

Ephesians 4:26 says, "be ye angry and sin not: let not the sun go down upon your wrath." Christians don't have to agree on everything; spiritual growth and understanding can come through disagreements. When what we believe is challenged and remain unchanged, the confidence in that belief soars. On the other hand, if our belief is proven to be incorrect, we should forsake our pride and abandon our initial belief for the greater truth.

David's belief was challenged in a similar manner in 1 Samuel 23. David asked God if he should attack the Philistines because they were looting the city of Keilah. God commanded him to save Keilah. David relayed the message to his men, but they were fearful and did not want to face the Philistines on the battlefield. What followed is a lesson for anyone who wants to be a good spiritual leader.

David went back and inquired of the Lord again. David didn't take the concerns of the people as a threat to his leadership or as an act of insubordination. Because the people were not in agreement, David wanted to confirm that he was following God's instruction. In this case, God confirmed His previous direction.

David went to assist Keilah, and his men went with him. David understood that he was not perfect nor did he have perfect understanding. He was sensitive to the fact that God, at times, speaks wisdom through others to right our path. David restored the confidence of his men by simply praying again.

War is sometimes necessary, but the weapons of a believer's warfare are not of this world. They are spiritual and mighty through God to dismantle the schemes and to destroy the strongholds of our enemy (2 Corinthians 10:4). Spiritual wars, when they are quick and handled properly, will serve to increase our depth and breathe of knowledge.

Whether spiritual or physical, a quick war minimizes casualties and allows for a speedy return to development and reconstruction. For instance, marriages that are "war-like" without interludes of peace are often under-cultivated, underdeveloped, and short-lived. Frequent fights, petty differences, and irrational suspicions all take a toll and prevent the couple from constructing the masterpiece their marriage is supposed to be.

The closest a person can expect to come to doing both, warring and building at the same time, is doing one while preparing for the other. Each builder had a sword fastened to his side during the construction of the city walls of Jerusalem (Nehemiah 4:18). While building the wall, they were prepared of war. David did the opposite; he warred against the enemies of Israel while preparing to build the temple. There is a season for everything (Ecclesiastes 3:1), and knowing when to swing a sword versus when to swing a hammer can make all the difference.

Chapter 6

DIVINE DESTINY

The idea that every person is tied to a specific destiny, a predetermined fate, can provide both relief and a sense of helplessness. There is peace in knowing that our future cannot be thwarted by bad decisions or outside influences. It can also make us feel helpless to escape a destiny that is not desirable.

Paul introduced the term "predestined" to the doctrine of salvation (Ephesians 1:5, 11), implying to some that the redeemed among us are pre-conditioned to walk a preexistent path to a pre-ordained future. This is welcome news to those who regularly join their congregation in worship (Hebrews 10:25) and practice their faith daily. To others, this is a difficult concept to grasp. It is difficult for someone to accept that a loved one who dies without Christ will not be chosen by God to be among the multitude of saints John saw in his vision of heaven (Revelation 7:9).

The idea that God writes our destiny from beginning to end is incongruent with a primary principle of salvation: we all have free will, the power to make our own decisions. Adam was not destined to disobey God, he chose to disobey God. His disobedience impacted his destiny.

How just can God's plan of salvation be if we are but pawns, involuntarily moved to and fro without an appreciable role in shaping our future? A God that has no respect of persons (Romans 2:11) could not justifiably map out a path to salvation for some and not others. There must, therefore, be a discriminator between the two, and the discriminator is the free-will choice to accept Jesus Christ as Savior and Lord.

In this chapter, we will deal with this complex topic. We explore the possibility of changing our destiny, foreseeing our destiny, and pursuing our destiny. Moreover, we will examine prayer, prophecy, and predestination. Prayer, when enriched with faith, has the power to amend our destiny. Prophecy, when given by God, is endowed with the power to reveal our destiny. Predestination is solely in the hands of God who secures our divine destiny.

PRAYER

Prayer stands among man's most sacred acts, a duty of all believers. The heroes of faith from Genesis to Revelation understood the power of prayer as an agent of change and instiller of strength. In Genesis 20:17, God healed the barren women of Abimelech's house in response to Abram's prayer. Once without a place in perpetuity, the fate of Abimelech's linage was changed forever. Abraham's answered prayer typifies countless biblical accounts where men and women of God prayed and things changed: Droughts ended, the dead lived again, fire rained from heaven, the sun stood still, and an entire city repented. Prayer brings us closer to the God we serve and reveals the person we often hide within ourselves.

If Jesus, the son of God, found it necessary to pray, then how much more should we? His disciples agreed with this sentiment and asked him, as recorded in Luke 11, "Lord, teach us to pray as John also taught his disciples." Note that the gospel of Matthew differs from Luke's on the placement of this moment relative to other events in Jesus' ministry. According to Matthew's gospel, the model prayer was provided as a part of Jesus' Sermon on the Mount (Matthew 6: 9-13) and not at the prompting of His disciples as found in Luke.

Matthew, in his gospel, put significant emphasis on capturing Jesus' perspective on the importance of prayer; however, Matthew only recorded two occasions where Jesus actually prayed (Matthew 14:23 and Matthew 26). In contrast, Luke painted a picture of Jesus' humanity, which was made evident by His need to pray. Luke, by including Jesus' prayers, placed special emphasis on His relationship with the Father. His gospel account provides inspiration for our approach to building a relationship with God through prayer.

Matthew encourages prayer through Jesus' exhortation, and Luke encourages prayer through Jesus' demonstration. Our discourse focuses on the latter. More specifically, we focus on the six times

Jesus prayed between His baptism and His disciples' request for instructions on prayer, as recorded by Luke.

Luke introduces us to the praying Jesus in chapter 3 during His baptism. The baptism marked the first day of His ministry, and the first day of His ministry was marked by prayer. Luke does not record Jesus praying during every miracle, but we are given another picture of Him in prayer, when He withdrew Himself from the fame and multitude who came to hear and be healed by Him (Luke 5:16). This was the second time the disciples witnessed the praying Jesus.

We glean several messages from these events. First, prayer precedes Godly work as seen with Jesus' prayer during His baptism. Second, God confirms the work He ordains. God said, "this is my beloved son in whom I am well pleased." Third, withdrawing to prayer counters the prideful pull of fame and human exaltation that can come with being an instrument of God. Jesus was gaining celebrity status. A multitude of people followed Him like the paparazzi. His popularity soared, but He would not allow His pride to do the same. What better way to humble one's self than prayer?

The attentive student can learn vital lessons from Jesus' approach to prayer: First, prayer should never be a ritual or something that is taught as though it is the next assignment on a syllabus. Second, prayer is sacred communication with God. Third, prayer is best taught when the desire to talk to God demands it.

Jesus demonstrated the importance of prayer until His disciples learned to appreciate its value. Jesus did what we should do when we aim to teach others. He simply did what He wanted them to do. Prayer was a frequent occurrence with Jesus. Luke 6:12 says, "...in those days, He went out into a mountain to pray, and continued all night in prayer to God." His commitment to prayer must have had a huge impact on how His disciples viewed it.

Jesus, in Luke 9, continued to demonstrate the value of prayer, working to create in the disciples a sincere desire to do the same. In verses 1 and 2, we see Jesus sending the disciples forth with power and authority to carry the kingdom message accompanied by miracles – note that this was done prior to teaching them to pray (Luke 11). The rest of the chapter brings prayer into focus in four distinct instances: prayer *multiplies* two fish and five loaves, *calibrates* Jesus with God's will, *transforms* Jesus from the natural to the spiritual, and *empowers* God-given power to fulfill God's purposes.

Prayer Multiplies

The disciples, in verse 16, watched Jesus as He took "five loaves and two fish, and looking up to heaven, He blessed them." This blessing turned out to be much more than the standard "God is great, God is good...Thank you for my food, Amen" prayer. When Jesus prayed in public, He indirectly taught His disciples to pray. His prayer at the gravesite of Lazarus brings this point to light. He said, "...I know that though hearest me always: but because of the people which stand by I said it...Lazarus, come forth" (Luke 11:42-43). The disciples were limited by what they saw and needed to learn the power of prayer as a catalyst to bring about the impossible.

By offering up what we have to God, we give what we have an opportunity to grow beyond the limits of its current destiny. A meal destined for one was rerouted by prayer to a destiny that fed a multitude. The power of prayer cannot be underestimated. The meal was big enough for the young boy it was meant to feed but too small for the multitude it needed to feed. When we look to God for help with our insufficiencies, He turns not enough into more than enough.

Unfortunately, like the disciples, our vision is limited. We are often thrust into situations that we are ill-equipped to handle. Inevitably, we all face circumstances that are beyond our ability to resolve, producing roadblocks that can block the path to our destiny. This is where prayer is invaluable. Prayer presents the opportunity for God to repurpose what we possess in a manner that opens our eyes to see a destiny greater than what we thought possible.

Prayer Calibrates

Prayer, in the purest sense, is talking to God; but, in the realest sense, it's the mechanism through which we naturally evoke or connect with a spiritual

God. Prayer is also a solitary encounter. Sure, we have corporate prayer, where we go to God in a unified manner. We pray together at the dinner table. We pray together on the National Day of Prayer. There are countless times when it is appropriate to pray with others. Nevertheless, prayer that is personal and genuine holds the unique power of calibrating our focus towards our God-ordained destiny.

In Luke 9:18, we read that "[Jesus] was alone praying." Luke goes on to note that "His disciples were with Him." How can one be alone and others with them? When we connect with God, whether in public or private, it's always in solitude. The disciples were physically present, but Jesus was alone with His Father. Jesus' time in prayer, as stated in Luke 9:18, was different from the prayer Jesus prayed at Lazarus' grave, where He prayed that those about Him might believe. Here, Jesus prayed in the presence of His disciples, yet He was alone.

The lack of details about this prayer suggests that perhaps Luke was out of earshot, or he wants us to focus on what happened following the prayer more than the prayer itself. After Jesus prayed, He began to press His disciples on who He was. He first asked them who others said He was and concluded by asking them who they thought He was. Everyone who spends time in prayer can attest to the fact that what is discussed with God during these solitary moments tends to leave thoughts that linger well after the prayer is over. Likewise, Jesus spent time in prayer and rose with a clear objective to prepare the disciples for His departure.

Jesus began to focus on the core aspects of the gospel, which He was destined to write with His life and the disciples were destined to share with the world. Furthermore, Matthew 16:21 tells us that Jesus, began to explain to His disciples that He would go to Jerusalem and suffer at the hands of the elders, chief priests, and scribes. He would be killed and raised from the dead on the third day. The disciples were not ready to understand who the Son of God was until He revealed Himself to them, and they were not ready to comprehend their destiny until they received the revelation that He was and is the Christ.

Reading the gospel accounts gives us the sense that Jesus was very busy. He was constantly interrupted by people seeking a cure for their infirmities. He was frequently challenged by people who were waiting for the Messiah but didn't recognize Him as He stood before them.

Life is filled with distractions, discouraging moments, and disturbing events. The time we spend in focused prayer helps us orient ourselves on the path to our destiny. In these private times, God shows us the past, present, and future: what has been left undone, what to do next, and what lies ahead.

Jesus used prayer to calibrate Himself to the will of God. At Lazarus' grave, He called on the power of God to restore life. As He completed His prayer in Luke 9, He led Peter to understand that the man that stood before him was the Christ, the Messiah (v. 21), the giver of eternal life.

Prayer Transforms

Once the disciples truly understood who Jesus was, they were ready for what was next. His instructions began to point to the future and challenge their commitment. He told them that suffering, rejection, and resurrection were in His near future. Suffering, He added, would be inescapable for those who followed Him toward His destiny. It was at this moment that the disciples were ready for a deeper understanding of God's will. As we move through the text in Luke, we see clearly that the Father and the Son agreed that the disciples were ready for what was next.

Eight days later, Jesus is shown praying again (Luke 9:28). This time, He took Peter, James, and John up a mount, the "Mount of Transfiguration," to pray (Matthew 17). The three disciples experienced in that moment an extraordinary understanding of who Jesus was, and He exposed them to an extraordinary view of the spiritual exchange that accompanied prayer. This prayer elevated Jesus spiritually and in the eyes of the disciples. It quickened Him towards His destiny and motivated the disciples to pursue a destiny greater than they previously envisioned.

Jesus in this moment of prayer demonstrated the power of prayer to change us. Prayer transfigures us, transforms us into something more beautiful, something elevated. Jesus was wholly holy. He was without sin; thus His transfiguration was an extraordinary thing to behold. "His countenance was altered, and His raiment was white and glistering,"

142

according to Luke 9:29. It is awesome to consider the idea that connecting with Heaven through prayer can make us more heavenly, in spirit, character, and countenance.

Jesus taught the disciples the importance of prayer by praying often; the power of prayer in multiplying two fish and five loaves of bread; and the calibrating capability of prayer in leading them to the revelation of Christ. Then, He taught them the transformative nature of prayer, which elevated what they perceived to be within the realm of possibility.

Witnessing Jesus' transfiguration elevated the disciples' imagination so much so that Peter concluded that they were underachieving. Walking around teaching and healing the sick was now beneath Jesus. Their view of Him changed dramatically. His status was elevated. He now stood in the company of the greatest Hebrew prophets, Moses and Elijah (Luke 9:33).

The disciples proposed to make three temples to solidify His place in history. Though misguided, their imagination was now limitless. Building three temples would not have been a small thing. It would have been a major undertaking for these men of meager means. An affluent group of men would not have complained about a woman wasting money in anointing Jesus with the oil from her precious alabaster box (Matthew 26:7) nor would they have considered betraying Jesus for thirty pieces of silver a good deal (Matthew 26:15) – this presumes that Judas would not have taken these actions if resources were bountiful. Jesus' disciples did not have an abundance of resources, yet Peter could envision building not one but three temples. With an active imagination, they were ready and willing to accept and pursue the impossible. Likewise, it is our job to imagine, and God will exceed, as well as guide, our imagination.

The philosopher and educator, Alfred North Whitehead, said, "Fools act on imagination without knowledge; pedants act on knowledge without imagination." Imagination is important but should be tempered with knowledge, a principle presented in the text before us.

God did not allow the disciples' imagination to run away with them (v. 35). He told them to listen to Jesus. The experience transformed their imagination, and listening to Jesus would provide the knowledge necessary to temper their imagination.

We look to Jesus, the Word of God, to calibrate our elevated imagination. The disciples' view of the transfigured Christ elevated their view of His divine destiny. During His transfiguration, Jesus was reminded of His departure from the earth in Jerusalem, which was His divine destiny. This is the message Jesus would carry forward to help the disciples map their imagination to their destiny.

Prayer Empowers

The next day, Jesus and the disciples came down from the mountain and was met by a crowd of people (v. 37). Luke made mention of one man in particular. This man had a son, which was tormented by an unclean spirit. He requested healing for his son but not without implicating the disciples, making it clear that he solicited their help, but they were ineffectual in casting out the spirit. Of course, Jesus healed the man's son.

Mark 9:28 tells a similar account and adds that the disciples – perhaps embarrassed about their inability to help the man who openly expressed his disappointment with their ineptitude – asked Jesus privately why they couldn't cast out the dumb and deaf spirit. He answered, "This kind can only come out by fasting and prayer." Without prayer and fasting, they were limited in their ability to do what Jesus gave them power to do.

Consider how Jesus prepared the apostles for this critical moment. They were presented with an opportunity to do what they were commissioned to do. Prior to the instance in Mark 9:28, Luke 9:1 tells us that Jesus "called the twelve disciples together, and gave them power and authority over all devils, and to cure diseases." We conclude that, although the disciples were given power over devils, power alone was not enough. The disciples had the power to relieve the man's child from his anguish, but he had to turn to Jesus to do what they couldn't. Why? The disciples were not empowered by prayer and fasting.

We must take care not to judge the disciples too harshly for their inability to dispense with the unclean spirit. After all, Jesus did not prepare them to deal with these types of spirits. We have seen, to this point, instance after instance where Jesus taught and demonstrated the importance of prayer, yet teaching His disciples to pray wouldn't come until Luke 11. The lesson here is significant.

Jesus did not fully equip them to do what He commanded them to do. First, they did not possess the power of prayer. Their understanding of prayer was not mature enough for them to desire it. Jesus said "we have not because we ask not," and here we find a perfect example. The disciples did not have the power of prayer because they had not asked for it. Furthermore, Jesus did not teach the disciples to pray until the desire to do so was mature enough to compel them to ask for instruction (Matthew 11:1).

Luke's emphasis on prayer is echoed in Jesus' cursory focus on the subject. Jesus frequently taught the importance of prayer, but He didn't teach His disciples to pray until they asked. In fact, John's disciple asked Jesus why His disciples didn't fast and pray (John 5:33, Mark 2:18, and Matthew 9:14), and Jesus simply answered by telling him and the others that gathered that His disciples did not need to fast. He did not, however, address the second part of their question: prayer. Jesus was clear that fasting was not necessary while He was on earth, but He did not conclude the same concerning prayer.

When empowered by prayer, we have power to change destinies. We know that Jesus spent ample time in prayer and was empowered by it. To do likewise is to add fuel to the fire that burns within us. As with the disciples, God grants the believer power and authority to accomplish what he/she is commissioned to do.

God gives us power to perform every task and fulfill every purpose He designs. The power we possess, however, is limited by the depth of our connection with God. Furthermore, our effectiveness in accomplishing God's will is directly correlated with our connection with Him. God gives us power to do great, impactful things, but the power is limited without prayer.

The disciples' inability to deliver the man's son was largely by Jesus' design. There are things we have power to accomplish, but Jesus reserves some things for Himself. The lack of success can't always be characterized as a failure. God choses some situations to handle Himself, yet it is never inappropriate to ask.

After teaching the disciples to pray in Luke 11, Jesus transitioned to a lesson He previously demonstrated, the principle of asking, seeking and knocking. First, Jesus taught the disciples to pray. Then, He told His disciples a parable about a man who asked a friend for three loaves in the middle of the night (Luke 11:8).

Friendship was not enough to get the man out of bed and risk waking up his children. However, the persistent plea of his friend was enough to make him "rise and give him as many [loaves] as he needed." Jesus, in Luke 18:6, revisited this idea of persistence in prayer with a parable about a widow's supplication to an unjust judge. Never underestimate the value of asking God for what the heart desires.

Next, He told them to ask, seek, and knock. It is intuitive to present request-filled prayers. We, more often than not, pray because we need God to do what we can't, but prayer is much more than stringing together a list of desperate desires. The friend in need of loaves and the widow who went before the unjust judge did much more than ask. They were seekers and knockers.

We are expected to ask for what we don't have, seek what we don't know, and knock when we don't have access. The power of prayer to impact our destiny is in our willingness to cultivate it. Prayer should be continuous and not something we do as needed. Persistent seeking and knocking calibrates and empowers our asking. When life seems to be going in the wrong direction, ask for clarity, seek His will, and knock to gain access to your divine destiny.

PROPHECY

Have ye not seen a vain vision, and have ye
not spoken a lying divination, whereas ye say,
The Lord saith it; albeit I have not spoken?
Ezekiel 13:7

Prophecy, the prediction of future events, is a powerful tool God employs to point man's faith towards Himself. Jesus, in John 14:28-29, told His disciples about His impending death and return. In particular, He said, "...I have told you before it come to pass, that, when it is come to pass, ye might believe." Faith and human belief are the principle targets of prophecy.

The Bible contains over forty prophecies of the coming, crucifixion, and return of the Messiah. These prophetic passages, which are presented in various ways, predict the extension of God's grace towards mankind through His son. It is by the fulfillment or realization of these events we are assured that Jesus was and is the Messiah. Jesus, who proved to be the embodiment of prophecies made well before His birth, stands as our hope for the future. This hope is born of faith; faith erected in the wake of God's glorious transition of prophecy into our contemporary reality.

The most significant prophecy is found in Isaiah 58:

> 2. For he shall grow up before him as a tender plant, and as a root out of a dry ground: he hath no form nor comeliness; and when we shall see him, there is no beauty that we should desire him.
> 3. He is despised and rejected of men; a man of sorrows, and acquainted with grief; and we hid as it were our faces from him; he was despised, and we esteemed him not.
> 4. Surely he hath borne our griefs, and carried our sorrows: yet we did esteem him stricken, smitten of God, and afflicted.

5. But he was wounded for our transgressions, he was bruised for our iniquities: the chastisement of our peace was upon him; and with his stripes we are healed. 6. All we like sheep have gone astray; we have turned everyone to his own way; and the Lord hath laid on him the iniquity of us all.
7. He was oppressed, and he was afflicted, yet he opened not his mouth; he is brought as a lamb to the slaughter, and as a sheep before her shearers is dumb, so he openteth not his mouth.
8. He is taken from prison and from judgement: and who shall declare his generation? For he was cut off of the land of the living: for the transgression of my people was he stricken.
9. And he made his grave with the wicked, and with the rich in his death; because he had done no violence, neither was any deceit in his mouth.

This prophecy foretells the life, death, and burial of Jesus. God allowed Isaiah to see and foretell the life of the Messiah. In so doing, our faith in Jesus as the Messiah is founded on seeing what was revealed to Isaiah. Jesus did not adjust His destiny to match prophecy. Rather, prophecy became confirmation of His destiny and vice versa. In like manner, the believer's destiny is secured through the fulfillment of the Messianic prophecies. His death, burial, and resurrection provides a fork in the road for all to accept a new destiny that leads to eternal life or maintain a course towards destruction.

For "as many as received Him, to them gave He power to become the sons of God, even to them that believe on His name" (John 1:12).

Only prophets that say what they see will see what they say. Prophets do not possess the power to design the destiny of another. God gives prophets a glimpse of the future, and the words of a true prophet are destined to become a contemporary reality unless the destiny is disrupted by a repentant heart.

The destiny revealed at the time a prophecy is given may be absolute and accurate, yet not immutable. Some prophesies are given as a warning to those who need a course correction. Jonah and Hezekiah are prime examples.

God gave Jonah a glimpse of Nineveh's destiny of destruction (Jonah 1:1-2), yet He reconstructed the destiny of Nineveh after they repented and "turned from their evil way" (Jonah 3:10). The king and people of Nineveh were not only repentant but made a great show of their repentance through fasting and prayer. Everything that breathed, even the animals, honored God with a fast.

For Nineveh's actions, they obtained the grace of God.

In like manner, Isaiah revealed to Hezekiah his destiny, which was an impending death (Isaiah 38:1). This prophecy was also short-lived. With a sincere prayer, Hezekiah cashed in his faithfulness to God, which turned out to be worth fifteen more years of life.

In the case of Nineveh, God forgave. In the case of Hezekiah, God showed mercy. Both received a prophecy that foretold an undesirable destiny, but their futures were altered through sincere prayer. No one's destiny is set in stone, not even when it is the object of prophecy.

Seeing What You Say

Prophecy is less about what the prophet knows and more about what God sees. Our destiny lies at the focal point of what God sees as He looks back at us from some point in the future. God doesn't just see who we are. He sees who we will become. The course we set influences our destiny, and our willingness to do what is necessary to improve our destiny is limited by our ability to envision a destiny greater than what we see.

Jonah arrived at Nineveh with extremely bad news: In forty days, the city would be overthrown (Jonah 3:4). The king of Nineveh could have accepted or disregarded the prophecy. He chose neither. He decided to appeal to God to change Nineveh's destiny. The king enacted a decree on several fronts. His intent was clear, "Who can tell if God will turn and repent, and turn away from His fierce anger, that we perish not?" The king hoped that God would see their fasting and hear their prayer and grant them an alternate future. How can we experience a better future unless we first open our hearts to envision an alternate destiny?

Our vision is most often limited by our current state of affairs. Consider Abram, in Genesis 15, as God changes his destiny and gives him the promise of a great legacy. This is the defining moment of Abram's life. We cannot fully understand Genesis 15 without the pre-textual context provided in Genesis 14:22-23. Abram did not accept gifts offered to him by the king of Sodom. His reason? He would not embrace a destiny where the king could say, "I made Abram rich." After Abram displayed such sound judgement and character, God determined to reward him. Abram's concern, however, was that he had no heir to leave his inheritance. His current state of affairs limited his ability to envision what God saw.

Abram resolved that his childless destiny would end with Eliezer, his servant. Without an heir, his estate was destined to establish another man's legacy. What Abram saw shaped what he believed; therefore, God aimed to change what he saw. How did he accomplish this? He removed him from the things that, to this point, defined his destiny. He took him outside, away from his house, servants, and family in order to help him accept his true destiny.

Abram defined his destiny by what he saw in the horizontal. God wanted Abram to define his destiny by what he saw in the vertical. Thus, he took Abram outside (Genesis 15:3) to change his perspective. Once outside, God told him to look up. Only after he looked towards the heavens could he see the sign of his divine destiny. Seeing the canvas of heaven speckled with an innumerable collection of stars assisted Abram in embracing his divine destiny through a perspective only God could provide.

Prophecy is the ability to see what God sees. Abram believed God once he was able to see what God saw. David's father, Jesse, could only see a shepherd boy (1 Samuel 16), but God saw a King. Pharaoh's daughter saw a Hebrew baby on the Nile River (Exodus 2:6), but God saw Moses, an instrument of Israel's deliverance. The early Church saw Saul (Acts 9:13), an abuser of Christians, but God saw Paul, an Apostle of Jesus Christ. One's divine destiny cannot be charted based on signs perceived through natural means; it is revealed to us when God shows us what He sees.

Prophesying with Purpose

Prophecies are given with a purpose, so we might believe and grow in faith. Ultimately, prophecies were given so we could see a child in a manger, yet believe that He was destined to be our savior. The child in the manger could not save us, but His divine destiny was to pave the way for a destiny that supersedes all others, the salvation of the human race. Therefore, His destiny led Him to an unjust death, which gives us the opportunity to be justified by faith and experience the power of His resurrection.

God desires for everyone to experience the gift of salvation, and the foretelling of Jesus' life, death, and resurrection was provided so faith could perform a perfect work in those who believe. Humanity's free will is responsible for countless and sometimes lengthy detours from God's path and plan, but He always finds a way to make "all things work together for [our] good" (Romans 8:28). He turns bad to good and good to great. Imagine how much more impactful our lives would be if we sought to know the plans God envisions for us (Jeremiah 29:11).

Paul, in 1 Corinthians 14, spends an entire chapter discussing the value of prophesy versus speaking in an unknown tongue while in cooperate worship. He teaches us that prophecy is vital to the believer's development. It is good for edification, exhortation, and comfort. Having a God-given perspective builds us up, draws us near, and consoles us in light of the glaring contradictions between what we may be experiencing and the divine destiny prophesied concerning us. Thus, Paul advises that we should earnestly desire to prophesy (v. 39), and by virtue, we all should seek to see what God sees.

Prophesying with Consistency

Those who aspire to prophesy should be mindful that God only fulfills prophecy that works towards His purposes. God, not the prophet, is the source of prophecy. Therefore, the underlying expectation of all prophecy is that the origin is supernatural and not the product of human imagination. The Holy Scripture gives instances, patterns, and types, which are meant to assist in understanding God's character through His previous actions. Therefore, prophecies given by God will always be consistent with the promises of scripture.

The importance of getting prophecy correct cannot be overstated. Prophecies are given as a means to increase our faith, the thing without which we cannot please God (Hebrews 11:6). Incorrect prophecies suggest that God is ineffective in keeping His word. False prophecy engenders doubt in the heart of the hearer and is such a serious matter that it is considered a crime worthy of death (Deuteronomy

18:20). This is the sentiment of Ezekiel 13:3, "Woe unto the foolish prophets, that follow their own spirit, and have seen nothing!" All are blind to the future; only God can give prophetic sight and insights.

During Jesus' journey to Bethsaida (Mark 8:21), He encountered a blind man who desired to see. Jesus could have healed him where he stood, but He took him out of town. As with Abram, taking him out of town changed his perspective. Jesus spat on the ground, touched him, and asked if he could see anything. The man said, "I see men as trees, walking." Jesus put His hands on him again and the man saw clearly.

Like the blind man Jesus encountered in Bethsaida, those who prophesy must not just seek to see what God sees. They must seek to see clearly. The man could initially see what Jesus saw, but he could not see it how Jesus saw it. Could it be that Jesus took him out of town because the man would have been excited about the improvement in his sight and perhaps satisfied with being nearsighted? Prophecy is not nearsighted; it sees afar off. Furthermore, prophecy that engenders faith must be precise, clear, specific, and come from God.

Amos 3:8 says it best: "The lion hath roared, who will not fear? The Lord God hath spoken, who can but prophesy?" The fear that grips the heart when hearing a lion roar is as natural as prophesying upon hearing God speak. God holds the secrets of our divine destiny and reveals it as He wills. Knowing God, when and how He speaks, is critical to ensuring that our prophetic moments serve to enhance the faith of believers as well as unbelievers as we are moved by the Holy Ghost (2 Peter 1:21).

PREDESTINATION

For I know the thoughts that I think toward
you, saith the Lord, thoughts of peace, and not
of evil, to give you an expected end.
Jerimiah 29:11

John Calvin, a French theologian during the Protestant Reformation of the 1500s, espoused the doctrine of predestination, which "affirms that despite evil and suffering, the ultimate destiny of the world and history rest in the good and infallible hands of God" (Kee et al. 1998). Since we believe the scripture is the ultimate authority in the believer's life, we examine the doctrine of predestination in light of what we find in Bible.

Paul familiarizes us with the term "predestinate" in Romans 8:29, but Jeremiah introduced the idea well before Paul coined the term. Jeremiah recounts the word of the Lord that came to him, which proclaimed that God knew him before he was formed in his mother's womb, sanctified him before he was born, and appointed him to be a prophet (Jeremiah 1:5). Jeremiah was unique among men. The omniscient God knew him before he was conceived in his mother's womb. God knew Jeremiah's end from the beginning of time and his beginning from the end of time. The omniscient God exists in and knows the past, present, and future simultaneously.

God knowing Jeremiah in this way does not make Jeremiah unique, however. What makes him so unique is his appointment as a prophet before he was born. Another person, as outlined in scripture, shared this distinction of being known, sanctified, and ordained before He was born.

Jesus, "Who verily was foreordained before the foundation of the world," was predestined for a specific purpose as was Jeremiah (1 Peter 1:20). Qualifying actions were not required for God to grant

Jesus and Jeremiah their respective, divine destinies. John, without using the word "predestined," points to Jesus' destiny as the "Lamb slain from the foundation of the world" for the propitiation of our sins (Revelation 13:8). Most other biblical examples were chosen by God based on how they compared with their generational peers.

Predestined not Predetermined

There are several biblical examples where God chose people and endowed them with a special purpose. Each were introduced to their divine destiny in response to their character at a time of God's choosing. Three people come immediately to mind.

First, Noah lived in a generation where "the wickedness of man was great in the earth...but Noah found grace in the eyes of the lord...Noah was a just man and perfect in his generations and Noah walked with God" (Genesis 6:5, 8, 9). Second, Abram was not chosen at birth; he was seventy five years old (Genesis 12:4). Third, David's kingship was not revealed to the prophet Samuel at his birth; David was a young man old enough to tend to his father's sheep (1 Samuel 16:11-13).

Noah, Abram, and David were chosen by God at specific times in their lives. Their divine destinies were not known to them at birth nor mapped out in advance. They were set on the course God planned for them at a time of His choosing and when they were ready to yield to His will.

Very few are appointed to a predetermined destiny. Most are chosen based on attributes suitable to God's will and plan. Saul, for example, was passionate about stopping the spread of the gospel message and was well known as a persecutor of the early church. However, his attitude changed, along with his name, once he accepted and experienced new life in Christ. Saul, now called Paul, did not change his passion; He simply redirected it. He became just as passionate about his divine destiny, spreading the gospel of Jesus Christ.

Let's take another look at Paul's use of the term "predestination" in Roman 8:29-30. Note that he sandwiched the promise of predestination between two significant points: "...all things work

164

together to them that love God..." and "if God be for us, who can be against us?" Paul used this section of scripture to encourage believers to stay the course during difficult times. First, God postures everything to work favorably for believers. Second, God predestines believers to be conformed to the image of His Son. Third, God is the believer's strong defense until his/her divine destiny is complete.

The context of Romans 8 does not lend itself to the idea that God predetermines the life of believers. The God who knows all could simply ensure bad things never happen rather than fixing things to work for our good. Even though God foreknows our dilemmas, He only predesigns solutions in response to His foreknowledge of our faith. He doesn't pre-ordain who will believe in the saving power of His son. He does, however, have perfect foreknowledge of those who will exercise their faith and be conformed into the image of His Son.

Predestined to Grace

Predestination does not dilute the power of faith nor the grace of God. God's holistic plan predestined us to be the children of God through the divine destiny of Christ "who works out everything in conformity with the purpose of His will" (Ephesians 1:11). Since it is His will for "all men to be saved," as Paul stated in 1 Timothy 2:4, why wouldn't He predestine all to be saved? Let's consider this question in light of Paul's letter to the Ephesians.

God predestined Christ to be sin's eternal sacrifice to restore mankind to Himself. He also predestined "us in Him before the foundation of the world, that we should be holy and without blame before Him in love." Furthermore, through the predestination of Christ, we were predestined to be the adopted children of God. By His grace, we are made acceptable to God despite our sin (Ephesians 1:4-6).

Our divine destiny is not separate from Christ's but rather a byproduct of having a predestined savior. God sacrificed His only son so that whosoever believes in Him could unlock their divine destiny (John 3:16). Jesus' death, burial, and resurrection were accomplished to usher in God's perfect will. We are all predestined to have access to

God, but only those who exercise faith towards Him will experience the grace-born destiny prepared for those who believe.

God has placed each person on a collision course with their divine destiny. All will inevitably come to a fork in the road where they must choose to accept God's divine destiny or some other path. Paul wisely chose his predestined path, and God used his passion to convert others. Peter, a fisherman, chose his predestined path, and God used his boldness to lead disciples in fishing for men. God does not predestine who we are; he predestines who we will become. Moreover, He uses who we are now to shape who we will become.

Chapter 7

THE MINISTRY OF RECONCILIATION

And all things are of God, who hath reconciled
us to himself by Jesus Christ, and has given to
us the ministry of reconciliation:
2 Corinthians 5:18

Every member of the body of Christ has a
role to play. 1 Corinthians 12 tells us that each part
of the body is as important as the next. If one part
does not or cannot perform its duties, then the body
becomes impaired. Though the body can still
function, it can never reach its full potential without
every member performing its duty. The
responsibility of each member can be referred to as
the member's ministry. In this chapter, we highlight
the ministry that the whole body has in common.

LIVING UNTO HIM

In 2 Corinthians 5:14, Paul asks a rhetorical question, "...if one died for all, then were all dead." He answered his question in Romans 5:17, "For if by one man's offence death reigned by one; much more they which receive abundance of grace and of the gift of righteousness shall reign in life by one, Jesus Christ." Adam's sin authored spiritual death for all mankind, but Christ authored life for everyone born under the curse of sin. The next verse outlines His expectation for us in response to His death.

> And that he died for all that they which live
> should not henceforth live unto themselves,
> but unto him which died for them, and rose
> again.
> 2 Corinthians 5:15

Accepting Christ places us in the category of the "they which live." In John 10:10, Jesus said, "...I am come that they might have life, and that they might have it more abundantly." Jesus promises that all can live and not only live but live a good life. We can live a prosperous life. Paul takes this idea of abundant life and combines it with a statement recorded in the fourteenth chapter of Luke. In verse 33, Jesus said, "So likewise, whosoever he be of you that forsaketh not all that he hath, he cannot be my disciple." Jesus offers us abundant life but expects us to live it for him.

Christ died so we can have life and the opportunity to commune and have a close relationship with God. In this life, we can have an abundance of joy and peace. This is a great deal for the receiver because there is little to no effort required to obtain it. The believer needs only to believe. God, on the other hand, provides for our every need and covers ever expense – what a high price he paid.

No one likes to see an expensive gift misused or wasted. When we pay a substantial amount for an item, we are very protective of it. I know this first hand as my music keyboard falls in the expensive category. No one is allowed to touch it unless they first are told how to properly handle it. They must receive instructions as to which buttons to push and which are off limits.

Many of us have such items, whether expensive in monetary or sentimental value. It may be a car that has certain idiosyncrasies that all drivers must be familiar with else it will not function properly. Maybe its electronic equipment that children are not allowed to touch until they are properly trained. Perhaps its cookware that requires special care. If we value it, we protect it. Christ takes a similar approach to handling His prize possession.

Jesus places great value on the life He's given us. He purchased our salvation and has placed a precious "treasure in [these] earthen vessels" (2 Corinthians 4:7). His intent is to dissuade us from misusing and abusing it. How does He plan to accomplish this? He employs the approach we use to protect the things we value. He simply teaches us to live our lives as He did.

Christ wants us to take the life He freely gives and live it according to His will. Followers of Christ should live the life He has given by His rules. Of course, the habits of our dead existence often make our transition to life a difficult one. Those who are accustomed to propping their feet up while watching television will struggle to keep their feet on the floor when visiting the home of a friend. Likewise, our habits and tendencies can make living unto God quite the struggle. However, it is a struggle we must win.

Failure only comes when we refuse to combat our undesirable habits and tendencies.

RECONCILED TO RECONCILE

Each member of the body of Christ must decide henceforth to live "unto Him which died for them." Then and only then will the collective body be able to fully execute its ministry. What is the ministry? It is the most important of all ministries, the ministry that goes beyond culture, doctrine, and denomination. It is the ministry is reconciliation.

> And all things are of God, who hath reconciled us to himself by Jesus Christ, and hath given to us the ministry of reconciliation;
> 2 Corinthians 5:18

All who believe in Christ become new creatures, and God makes all things new (2 Corinthians 5:17-18). We become disciples of Christ who live unto Him and not ourselves. God orchestrated our new-creature status by reconciling our souls to Himself through Jesus. Our reconciliation by Jesus Christ was the climax of His earthly ministry, thereby mending the broken relationship that developed when Adam sinned.

God's plan did not require Jesus to physically remain on earth to reconcile every person back to Himself. Instead, God sent Jesus to begin the process and gave the ministry of reconciliation to those who have been reconciled. This idea is continued in verse 19.

> To wit, that God was in Christ, reconciling the world unto himself, not imputing their trespasses unto them; and hath committed unto us the word of reconciliation.
> 2 Corinthians 5:19

Paul reemphasizes that the act of reconciliation was an exclusive action of God. Through the death of Christ, He completed the actions necessary for our spiritual reconciliation. Because of the reconciliation enacted by Jesus, God dropped all charges of sin and trespass. Finally, those who are reconciled have been entrusted with the word of reconciliation. They are responsible for relaying to others that "God was in Christ, reconciling the world unto himself, not imputing their trespasses unto them."

THE WORD OF RECONCILIATION

You are our epistle written in our hearts,
known and read of all men: Forasmuch as ye
are manifestly declared to be the epistle of
Christ ministered by us, written not with ink,
but with Spirit of the living God; not in tables
of stone, but in fleshy tables of the heart.
2 Corinthians 3: 2-3

Paul referred to the saints at Corinth as epistles and suggested that they were saved through his preaching and teaching. Because the Corinthians knew Paul, there was no needed for an introduction or a review of his credentials. Their life in Christ and commitment to the faith was not only evidence of their salvation but also of his credibility as a man of God.

If the saints at Corinth could be ambassadors for Paul, then surely our lives should speak for Christ. The old expression says, "Christians are the only Bible some may ever read," so, if that is the case, we must make every effort to ensure what they read is a proper representation of our love for Christ.

Paul was not taking credit for the Corinthians' salvation. In verse 5, he stressed the part he was privileged to play in it. "We are not sufficient of ourselves to think anything as of ourselves," he said. When we do our part in reconciling others to God, we must remember that He is the one who ultimately draws and saves. We are but ministers of the new testament.

> Who also hath made us able ministers of the new testament; not of the letter, but of the spirit for the letter killeth, but the spirit giveth life.
> 2 Corinthians 3:6

Paul's mention of the new testament in the above scripture is not a reference to the biblical canon we use today. By new testament, he means the new covenant, the covenant of love, the gospel of Jesus Christ, the word of reconciliation.

We are not to just be ministers but able ministers. Able ministers, according to 2 Corinthians 3:6, have a distinct and proper approach to scripture. Understanding Paul's distinction between the letter and spirit provides the framework for understanding the entire Bible, both Old and New Testaments. Scripture is most often misinterpreted when we fail to view it within the framework of the letter versus the spirit.

The Letter Killeth

It is common to refer to the letter as the Law or the letter of the Law. Rarely do we approach the New Testament in the same manner as the Old Testament. Most believers, who embrace the doctrine of the New Testament, do not strictly follow the laws of the Old Testament. It is true that the New Testament ushered in the dispensation of grace, which relieves us from the rites and edicts of the Law. However, attempting to follow the New Testament verbatim makes it as legalistic as doing so with the Old Testament.

> All scripture is given by inspiration of God,
> and is profitable for doctrine, for reproof, for
> correction, for instruction in righteousness:
> That the man of God may be perfect,
> thoroughly furnished unto all good works.
> 2 Timothy 3:16-17

The above passage is taken from one of the letters Paul wrote to Timothy, his young protégé. It is easy to see how someone could unwittingly quote this scripture in reference to the Old and New Testament. Paul, however, could not have been referencing any New Testament scripture since it had not yet been compiled as we know it today.

Although God inspired the writings of the New Testament, Paul did not account for them here.

The law "was ordained to life...and is holy and the commandment holy and just, and good" (Romans 7:10, 12). The law, as stated in the Old Testament, is not outdated by any means. We cannot choose to keep the laws that are palatable and throw out the rest. We are prone to do this because the law is extremely demanding in some cases. However, the idea that the law is too demanding is a misconception.

Both the Old and New Testaments, in their entirety, are valuable to the growth and development of believers. When the disciples spread the Christian faith, they did it via the law and the prophets. Today, we almost exclusively use the New Testament. We teach that we are in the dispensation of grace as though the New Testament takes precedence. This excuse does not hold because the early church lived in the same dispensation. Look at the following example:

> And when they had appointed him a day, there came many to him into his lodging; to whom he expounded and testified the kingdom of God, persuading them concerning Jesus, both out of the law of Moses, and out of the prophets, from morning till evening.
> Acts 28:23

The scripture is clear as to the references Paul used to testify of the kingdom of God. Philip preached Jesus to the Eunuch from the prophet Isaiah (Acts 8:30). The use of the Old Testament was a common practice in the early stages of the ministry of reconciliation. Therefore, when Paul said, *"the letter killeth,"* he could not have been implying that the Old Testament was a weapon of death.

The Spirit Giveth Life

To understand the word of God, we must understand the spirit of the word. To understand the spirit of the word is to understand the purpose of the word, the reason it was said or written. Once we understand the intent of scripture, the Spirit allows us to apply it accurately.

Although the New Testament was written for our edification, living it word-for-word will not lead us to fulfill what God intended. We must consider the scripture, audience, context, and the expected

179

result; then, we will find the spirit of the scripture or the lesson the scripture is designed to teach. Jesus said He did not come to destroy the law, but to fulfill it (Matthew 5:17). He did not throw it away; He condensed it.

> Jesus said unto him, Thou shalt love the Lord thy God with all thy heart, and with all thy soul and with all thy mind. This is the first and great commandment. And the second is like unto it, thou shalt love thy neighbor as thyself. On these two commandments hang all the law and the prophets.
> Matthew 22:37-40

Jesus considered the scripture, audience, context, and intent and summed up all thirty-nine books of the Old Testament in two statements. Consider the Ten Commandments. The first four teach us how to love God. The last six teach us how to treat each other. Now, consider the audience and context. God is speaking to the children of Israel, a rebellious people who grew up in communities among a plethora of idol worshipers. Next, consider the intent or purpose for the commandments. God gave guidelines to teach the Israelites how to interact with God and their neighbors.

Jesus simply extracted the principle/spirit of the scripture and made two seemingly new commandments. The spirit of the word says if you love God, you will not have any other gods before Him nor worship any other. Likewise, the spirit of the word says loving your neighbor like yourself means you will not steal from them, bear false witness against them, nor kill them.

This is what makes the word of God a living word. The Bible is filled with cultural and era references. These must be identified and put in perspective. Questions like, "Why did He say this?" and "What was He trying to accomplish by saying it?" must be asked. When we address these questions, we will be better equipped to apply the scripture to every situation.

THE MINISTRY IS YOURS

God committed unto us the ministry and the word of reconciliation. It is our responsibility to see that the world hears that there is a living and loving God who longs for fellowship. God wills that all men be saved and receive the blessings that come with salvation. This work or ministry is not reserved for a select few.

> And he gave some, apostles; and some,
> prophets; and some; evangelists; and some,
> pastors and teachers; For the perfecting of the
> saints, for the work of the ministry, for the
> edifying of the body of Christ:
> Ephesians 4:11-12

God has put gifted leaders among us to teach and encourage believers. Beyond that, He gifted them to equip believers to do the work of the ministry. Gifts are given so the body of Christ can understand and walk in the word and become epistles of flesh and ministers of reconciliation. Whatever the ministry, all have the responsibility of working towards the global ministry. The ministry of reconciliation is the spirit, goal, purpose, and reason for every word recorded from Genesis to Revelation.

The Great Commission

"Go ye therefore, and teach all nations, baptizing them in the name of the Father, and of the Son, and of the Holy Ghost: teaching them to observe all things whatsoever I have commanded you: and, lo, I am with you always, even unto the end of the world" (Matthew 28:19-20).

Chapter 8

THE POINT OF CONTENTION

The concept of eternal security can be divisive, not so much because of the complexity of the subject matter but the strong feelings tied to it. Either people become emotionally primed, or they refuse to talk about it due to the emotional tension the subject induces. Sometimes, after extensive deliberation and debate, they determine that further discussion is futile.

The idea of eternal security has divided the Christian community in two distinct camps, which is dangerous for many reasons. Jesus said, in Mark 3:24-25, "if a kingdom be divided against itself, that kingdom cannot stand. And if a house be divided against itself, that house cannot stand." These words were spoken in response to His accusers, who suggested that He dispelled devils by the power of the prince of devils. The power of eternal security to divide believers is the key reason we should proceed cautiously and deliberately.

My hope is to unify the body of Christ to whatever degree possible. However, everyone who reads this section will inevitably find a point of contention. It would be easy to omit this chapter, but a complete understanding of Christianity would not be possible unless eternal security is included in the dialogue.

Before you read on, understand that what I believe on the subject is far less important than what the scriptures say. With this in mind, we will examine scriptures which appear to support or refute the idea of eternal security. I am careful here to use the phrase "appear to" because it is impossible for scripture to give credence to both arguments. This too can be gathered from Mark 3:24-25. We will allow the preponderance of scriptural evidence to be our guide in ascertaining the appropriate conclusion to the matter.

ETERNAL SECURITY IS SCRIPTURAL?

In my years as a minister of the word, I've had the pleasure of discussing eternal security with a host of people from various backgrounds. During these discussions, I discovered that the proponents of eternal security consistently look to God's assurance that believers are "sealed" by the Holy Spirit. So, let's begin our examination of eternal security on this common ground: we are sealed. The Easton Bible Dictionary (1897) provides a well-laid-out definition, providing biblical usages of the term "seal."

> The use of a seals was mentioned in the New Testament only in connection with the record of our Lord's burial (Matthew 27:66). The tomb was sealed by the Pharisees and chief priests for the purpose of making sure that the disciples would not come and steal the body away (vv. 63, 64). The mode of doing this was probably by stretching a cord across the stone and sealing it at both ends with sealing-clay. When God is said to have sealed the Redeemer, the meaning is, that he has attested his divine mission (John 6:27). Circumcision is a seal, an attestation of the covenant (Romans 4:11). Believers are sealed with the Spirit, as God's mark put upon them (Ephesians. 1:13; 4:30). Converts are by Paul styled the seal of his apostleship, i.e., they are its attestation (1 Corinthians 9:2). Seals and sealing are frequently mentioned in the book of Revelation (5:1; 6:1; 7:3; 10:4; 22:10).

Easton's definition of seals can be grouped into two primary categories. They are used as a metaphor to highlight the authenticity of our association with God or as a securing mechanism used to prevent unauthorized access or exit. Moving forward, we will focus our attention on distinguishing the former from the latter, relying on scriptural context in an attempt to understand the implications of being sealed.

Sealed by the Holy Ghost

> Let no corrupt communication proceed out of your mouth, but that which is good to the use of edifying, that it may minister grace unto the hearers. And grieve not the Holy Spirit of God, whereby ye are sealed unto the day of redemption.
> Ephesians 4:29-30

Paul, in Ephesians 4, wrote to the church at Ephesus concerning their walk of faith. He urged them to walk worthy of the vocation wherewith they were called in order to maintain unity with the Spirit of God. He went on to say that the gifts given to man work towards this unity as well as the unity of the body of Christ.

He ends the chapter by urging his readers to forsake the old man, which was filled with uncleanness and greed and favor the new man, who is created after God in righteousness and true holiness. Before he ends, however, he cautions the church at Ephesus, in verse 30, not to grieve the Holy Spirit. For it is by the Holy Spirit that "[we] are sealed unto the day of redemption."

The question then becomes whether this is an authenticating or securing seal. The key is context. Is the writer using the phrase "you are sealed" to address the life changing power of the Holy Spirit or unchangeable power of salvation? If the latter is true, the chapter would have to focus on the power or strength of salvation to overcome our sinful nature. If the former is true, we expect Paul to make this statement in the context of spiritual growth. In fact, the chapter is just that, a call to spiritual growth.

Those who accept the verse as describing a securing seal must first accept the statement "you are sealed" as an arbitrary fact within the text. Paul spends the entirety of Ephesians 4 encouraging spiritual growth. He compels the reader to walk worthy of their calling (vv. 1-2), work towards unity (vv. 3-13), be mature in the faith (vv. 14-16), and put on the new man in Christ (17-32). Making the point that we are sealed or saved eternally in this context does not add to his appeal for unity and spiritual grown.

Paul used the same phrase "you were sealed" in the first chapter of Ephesians. Using the contextual argument here to categorize the statement as an authenticating or securing seal is not easily discerned. Paul's focus in Ephesians 1 is our new life in Christ. He says that God blessed us (v. 3), God predestined us (vv. 4-12), God saved and sealed us (vv. 13-14), he prayed for those God saved (vv. 15-18), and God is rich in glory, power, and authority. In chapter 1, he focused on God's role in our faith. In chapter 4, Paul focused on how we live our faith.

Those who see Ephesians 1:13 as pointing to an authenticating or securing seal can find support here. The contextual truth of the text could suggest that God predestined us to be saved from the foundation of the earth. Once saved, He sealed us. Whether He sealed us with His Spirit to identify us as His own or sealed us to ensure our place in Him throughout eternity, both are reasonable conclusions. One's predisposition tends to shift the balance of belief towards one or the other.

Let's take a closer look at both perspectives. The proponents of eternal security can view the seal of the Spirit as God's *proof* for the predestined believer, a gift "of our inheritance" to *validate* us until our salvation is completed in glory. Those who dispute eternal security can view the seal as God's *promise* to the predestined believer, a gift "of our inheritance" to *sustain* us until our salvation is complete in glory. In this context, both can be true. The seal marks us as God's property and locks us in the faith.

A word study of Ephesians 1:13; 4:30, Romans 15:28, and 2 Corinthians 1:22 also helps unravel the conundrum of eternal security. The transliteration of seal in the original text is sphragizó, which means to affix with a signet ring or other instrument, to stamp attesting ownership, or validating with a seal (Strong's, 4972). Armed with this definition, it becomes clear that Paul's use of the word "sealed" was clearly designed to articulate God's authentic ownership of the believer. Hence, we must conclude that pointing to the seal of the Spirit as God's mechanism to secure or lock the believer into salvation is a misrepresentation of Paul's intent.

The Good Shepherd will keep you

> My sheep hear my voice, and I know them,
> and they follow me: And I give unto them
> eternal life; and they shall never perish, neither
> shall any man pluck them out of my hand. My
> Father, which gave them me, is greater than
> all; and no man is able to pluck them out of
> my Father's hand.
> John 10:27-29

Proponents of eternal security also point to John 10:27-29 as clear evidence that salvation is a permanent state. Here we find Jesus during the Festival of Dedication in Jerusalem. While in the temple, Jews challenged Him to clearly state whether He was the Messiah. Jesus responded with a shepherd and sheep metaphor, in which He is the shepherd, and His disciples are His flock, given by the Father. The shepherd can keep his sheep, and no one can take them out of his hand. This may seem straight forward, but let's take a closer look.

There are several points to consider. First, His audience were Jews who heard His words and witnessed His works but did not believe: they were not His sheep (v. 25). Second, His sheep follow Him

(v. 27). Third, He gives His sheep eternal life (v. 28). Finally, no man can pluck His sheep out of His hand or the Father's (vv. 28, 29). In addition, there are distinct attributes of the sheep and the shepherd. The sheep hear His voice, are known of Him, and follow Him. The shepherd gives the sheep eternal life, no one can take the sheep from the shepherd, and the shepherd receives the sheep from the Father.

The metaphor set before us continues a series of parables used to articulate the relationship between the shepherd and his sheep. This was undoubtedly a difficult concept for the Jews to comprehend (John 10:5); thus, Jesus taught the same lesson three different ways: First, shepherds are contrasted with thieves that sneak into the sheepfold. The sheep follow the shepherd because they know his voice, but they do not know the voice of the thief and will not follow him (John 10:1-10). Second, Jesus compares himself, the Good Shepherd, to a hireling who abandons rather than protects the sheep when they are threatened by wolves (John 10:11-13). The third instance brings us back to where we began.

In each iteration of the parable, the shepherd, the protagonist, served as the protector of the sheep against the antagonist who clearly did not have the best interest of the sheep at heart. The antagonist was either a thief who will not enter the sheep fold by the door, a hireling who will not protect the sheep, or someone who would attempt to take the sheep away from the shepherd.

The third parable illuminated the first two; thus, it follows that we can gather a single truth from the key elements of them all. We first note that Jesus' sheep follow Him, and a stranger they will not follow. A stranger cannot convince the sheep to leave the fold because the sheep only trust the voice of the shepherd. Next, Jesus is the door to the sheepfold, and all sheep that enter through Him will be saved and have eternal life. Finally, wolves cannot scatter the sheep because the shepherd protects them.

What does this say about eternal security? The passage suggests that followers of Jesus will not follow another nor will they be chased out of the fold. This passage does not address sheep that stray away, but it is very clear that Jesus secures those He saves. He loves His sheep, even to the point of death. He will not allow anyone nor anything to steal, kill, or scatter them.

ETERNAL SECURITY IS NOT SCRIPTURAL?

Not Fit for the Kingdom of God

> And it came to pass, that, as they went in the way, a certain man said unto him, Lord, I will follow thee whithersoever thou goest. And Jesus said to him, Foxes have holes and birds of the air have nests; but the Son of man hath not where to lay his head. And he said to another, Follow me. But he said, Lord, suffer me first to go and bury my father. Jesus said to him, Let the dead bury their dead, but go thou and preach the kingdom of God. And another also said, Lord, I will follow thee; but let me first go bid them farewell, which are at home at my house. And Jesus said unto him, No man, having put his hand to the plough, and looking back, is fit for the kingdom of God.
> Luke 9:57-62

What type of disciple are you? Will you follow Jesus wherever He goes? Jesus, as He journeyed, encountered three would-be disciples. The first eagerly volunteered without apparent provocation. Jesus' response, however, suggests the consequences of such an open-ended commitment were not given much forethought. One must count up the cost before making such a hasty decision. Jesus does not resolve to make one rich or live lavishly. His premier purpose is to escort believers from death to life.

The second would-be disciple was beckoned, but had unfinished business. He desired to bury his father before committing to Christ. The Jewish custom required the immediate – or as soon as possible – burial of the dead, and the body to be guarded from death to burial (Greenberg 1981). Therefore, it is probable that the second man desired to return for an indefinite period to wait for his father to die and then bury him.

Jesus' priorities were different. The time to follow Him is always now. Waiting for death is far less important than seizing life. The spiritual prosperity that comes through following Christ should not be delayed. People who watch and wait to see how things will unfold before committing to Christ may miss their moment. Discipleship demands that we forget the things which are behind and press ahead (Philippians 3:13-14).

The third would-be disciple was trying to move in two different directions. He was caught between his desire to follow Jesus and his love for his family. He said, "Lord I will follow you," followed by "let me first go." He wanted to be a disciple, but he also wanted Christ to wait for him as he went in another direction. He attempted to dictate the terms of his discipleship. Jesus concluded that he was not ready. The focus of a good disciple cannot be divided.

A popular and widely accepted interpretation of Luke 9:62 is that anyone who begins a work for God and then looks back is not fit for the kingdom. This approach to the text suggests that the person was working for God then looked back. It seems more reasonable, however, that the "and looking back" describes an action during the act of reaching for the plow. The person who said, "Lord, I will follow You" was reaching for Christ, but was not willing to let go of his old life in the process. This view leads to the conclusion that Jesus was speaking more to the requirements for obtaining salvation than the possibility of losing it.

One is only ready to become a disciple of Christ or fit for the kingdom of God when they are willing to forsake all and follow Him. Jesus cautioned His disciples that denying themselves, taking up their cross, and following Him are conditions of discipleship. There is no such thing as a half-hearted disciple of Christ. Following Him requires a made up mind.

If We Faint Not

> But he that shall endure unto the end, the same
> shall be saved.
> Matthew 24:13

As Paul charged the church at Corinth, those in a race run the entire distance (1 Corinthians 9:24). Using a racing metaphor, he encouraged the church to do more than participate. We run to win. Those who run with confidence and keep pace are bound to finish. Paul infers that finishing the Christian race is certain for those who run (1 Corinthians 9:26), but in other instances his encouragement is to "faint not."

Paul, in Galatians 6:9, advocates for perseverance in doing good deeds. A worthwhile harvest awaits in the season set aside for reaping. The benefit of the labor put forth in the sewing season can only be fully appreciated during the harvest. As with any work, fatigue can become a factor when working for God. Paul understands this and cautions that we work until reaping season arrives. We can only reap "if we faint not."

What will we reap? We will reap what we sew (Galatians 6:7). Those who sew to, or serve, their own desires will reap corruption. Those who sew unto or serve the will of God will reap life everlasting. Paul iterates the principle of Romans 6:23, "For the wages of sin is death; but the gift of God is eternal life…" Therefore, Christians have the promise of eternal life, Paul adds, if we don't faint or give up.

Jesus saw the potential for His disciples, the apostles, to give up during perilous times (Matthew 24:13). He warned them of the difficult times ahead. They would be hated, afflicted, even put to death because of their belief in His name. They would live among traitors, enemies, false prophets, and the lascivious. Challenging times awaited them, but only those who were stubborn enough to "endure unto the end" would be saved.

Paul gives two reasons, in 2 Corinthians 4, why he didn't faint and why we shouldn't faint. In verse 1, he points to the ministry of reconciliation and the mercy of God as our sustaining force. Paul was committed to preaching the gospel of Jesus Christ and developing believers in response to God's enduring mercy. In verse 16, Paul reaffirms his resolve and refusal to faint in his efforts to cultivate life within the saints (v. 12). Although he was fatigued in his body, his spirit was renewed every day.

ETERNAL SECURITY DE-CONFLICTED

Who Can Achieve the Impossible

> For it is impossible for those who were once enlightened, and have tasted of the heavenly gift, and were made partakers of the Holy Ghost, And have tasted the good word of God, and the powers of the world to come, If they shall fall away, to renew them again unto repentance; seeing they crucify to themselves the Son of God afresh, and put him to an open shame.
> Hebrews 6:4-6

Next, we look at Hebrews 6:4-6 for further insight on eternal security. Christians tend to be divided between those who believe this passage describes 1) non-believers who were enlightened, and then fall away, and 2) believers who apostatize or renounce Christ. Let's put aside our preconceived notions, as best we can, and allow the scripture to speak freely.

We begin by breaking the passage into three parts: the subject (the enlightened), the action (the falling away), and the impossible task (the renewal unto repentance). Putting these together, we can derive the following phrase: "It is impossible for those who were once enlightened...if they should fall away, to renew them again unto repentance." In clearer terms, the enlightened who fall away cannot be renewed again to repentance.

The Enlightened

The book of Hebrews was written as a letter to Jewish converts who followed Christ. Some of these converts were considered to be immature in the faith (Hebrews 5:12). One of the themes of the book was to warn, instruct, and rebuke converts who were tempted to revert to Judaism or, in some cases "Judaize" the gospel – live out the gospel through Judaism. Furthermore, the passage refers to and describes the enlightened, which makes them genuinely born again believers rather than non-believers.

The King James Version precedes "enlightened" with "once were." This is very fitting since salvation is imparted not gained. We can neither meditate, pray, nor study until we become enlightened. We do not "become" enlightened at all. We "are" enlightened by the divine act of the Holy Ghost. This is the first indication that the enlightened in this passage are true believers.

The writer points to certain characteristics of the enlightened that affirm their status as believers. He states that the enlightened have tasted of the heavenly gift, which appears to be a reference to the grace of God. One can hear of the grace of God, but only a believer can experience it through salvation. Second, the enlightened are partakers of the Holy Ghost, a spiritual gift reserved only for believers.

Third, the enlightened have tasted of the good word of God, freedom from the law. Reading and hearing the word of God is not sufficient. "Oh taste and see that the Lord is good..." (Psalms 35:8). The consumption of the word leads to and cultivates the salvation of believers. Only through belief in Christ can the Law of Moses and the prophets be fulfilled in Jewish believers as well as gentiles. Finally, the enlightened have tasted of the powers to come. Again, only believers, citizens of heaven, are afforded heavenly peace and God's favor in this world.

The Falling Away

What do we do with the phrase "if they shall fall away?" Some point to this scripture as confirmation of eternal security, while others consider it a warning to believers not to turn away. The former believes this passage asserts that it is impossible for believers to fall away. The later sees this phrase as definitive proof that believers can withdraw from God and return to what they have forsaken.

We will refer to those who side with eternal security as "Lifers." Those who believe a person can fall away will be called "Resoluters." Lifers believe life once gained cannot be lost. Resoluters believe life once gained must be sustained through resolute faith in Christ.

Lifers are faced with difficult questions. At what point do we lose our free will? Do we lose the power of choice at the point of salvation? No. Submitting our will to God's will is a daily task. Paul said, "I die daily" (1 Corinthians 15:31). If we can choose to sin by not obeying the word of God, then turning from Him is a reasonable possibility.

Resoluters are faced with their own set of conundrums. How much sin does it take to lose our salvation? Better yet, can we sin away our salvation? No. Where sin abounds, grace much more abounds (Romans 5:20). There is no amount of sin that can undo or outdo the blood sacrifice made for us by the Son of God. Therefore, backsliding or falling back into old habits is not enough to disqualify us from the grace of God.

The Impossible

The impossibility in the passage is renewing someone to Christ through repentance after they have fallen away. The key word is repentance. Renewing a person again to repentance means changing their feelings towards Jesus. Furthermore, it is impossible to renew to repentance someone who disavows Jesus as the Son of God after gaining a full understanding of scripture and personally experiencing His goodness.

Falling away is not just falling back into sin or old habits. Falling away in this context refers to falling back into Judaism and denouncing Christ as the Messiah after receiving Him as the Savior. Those who receive Christ then return to serve idols or reject him as the only way to the Father put Him to an "open shame." In other words, they have tried and experienced Christ, but found their previous religion to be superior.

The expression "crucify again for themselves the Son of God, and put Him to open shame" is significant in that it was written to Jewish converts. It was the religious leaders who pushed for the crucifixion of Jesus, rejecting Him as the Son of God and prompting Pilate to put Him to an open shame. Therefore, a Jewish convert having personally experienced the saving grace of Jesus then turned back, choosing to renounce Him as the

Messiah, would have essentially realigned themselves with the accusing Jews.

In our pursuit of sound doctrine, we've examined a diverse group of scriptures related to eternal security, because doctrine must be more than scriptural. It must be biblical. Relying on one or two select passages of scripture to establish a doctrinal truth can lead to false doctrine. Only doctrine that holds true relative to every scripture in the bible can be considered "sound." Admittedly, we have not discussed every scripture related to eternal security, but the scriptures we have examined in this chapter steer us toward several conclusions.

We discovered that believers are sealed by the Holy Spirit, protected by the shepherding Son, fully committed, motivated by gratitude, and tempted with apostasy. True believers who yield to temptation and denounce Christ are lost forever, which makes eternal security a misnomer. Jesus warned that only those who endure to the end will be saved. Thus, the idea of eternal security is only applicable where faith in Christ remains.

Any born-again believer will testify, however, that "falling away," in the sense of committing apostasy, is not an option. The seal of the Holy Spirit is clear and distinct. God transforms believers through His Spirit and protects them as a shepherd protects his sheep. Only those who are fully committed receive His authenticating seal and enter into His sheepfold. His sheep know His voice, and the gratitude that floods their hearts will not allow them to follow another shepherd. Hence, apostasy is always possible but seldom probable. After all, who can experience the truth of God's love and grace today and denounce Him tomorrow?

Chapter 9

LIVING TO LIVE AGAIN

> If a man die, shall he live again? All the days
> of my appointed time will I wait, till my
> change come.
> Job 14:14

Pastor Isaac Bass, a distinguished older gentleman with a remarkable way with words, taught me that profound insight is best articulated with a conservative approach to communication. He and I met soon after his daughter and son-in-law arrived at the church where I had the privilege to pastor. Somehow, I managed to steal him away from his grandkids long enough to glean some advice and whatever life lessons he was willing to share.

I can't remember whether we went to breakfast, lunch, or just sat in my office and talked. However, I do remember the extraordinary impression he left on me with one simple statement.

He looked squarely into my eyes with the most sincere gaze and said, "Reverend," that's what Baptist preachers call each other, "I am living to live again."

Life after death is the blessed hope of the Christian faith. It is humanity's zenith of spiritual knowledge, the graduation from the university of natural life. Christians see death as the culmination of this life and the beginning of another. As the caterpillar transforms to a butterfly, death serves as a cocoon for the believer. Death is the vehicle by which we transition from temporal to eternal life. There are many merits to salvation, such as moral clarity, peace, and joy; however, the great hope of salvation is the resurrection.

THE RESURRECTION

The resurrection of the dead is God's final act of restoration. If salvation is a process, then the resurrection is its finale. Some enter the salvation process early and some late. Some endure the process for years and some finish almost as soon as they begin. The process is not equal in struggle nor reward. The process is sometimes misunderstood and misrepresented. The resurrection, however, is the one thing all believers can expect in full and equal measure. Salvation unravels without it.

Paul was a passionate apologist for the value of resurrection in the redemptive process. There were some in his generation who professed that "there is no resurrection of the dead..." and by implication, Christ was not risen (1 Corinthians 15:12, 13). Thus, he dedicated the entire chapter to contending for the resurrection of the dead as an indispensable truth, upon which the value of salvation hinges.

A Risen Savior

Salvation's distinguishing feature is the resurrection of Jesus. His resurrection is the principle prophecy among all predictions that solidify Him as the Messiah. Churches, sanctuaries, monasteries, hospitals, and community centers are built on the belief that Jesus is the Risen Savior. If He is not alive, then vain are the deeds we do in His name. Moreover, our faith in Him is useless, and we are not delivered from the power, penalty, and presence of sin. Paul states it this way in verse 17, "If Christ be not raised, your faith is vain; ye are yet in your sins."

Salvation hinges on three critical facts, and all must be true for the Christian faith to maintain biblical consistency. First, Jesus never committed a sin. The sacrifices of the Old Testament were required to be without blemish. The sacrifice had to be the best example possible in order to replace imperfection with perfection. Hence, Jesus, "did no sin" (1 Peter 2:22). He was the *perfect* sacrifice.

Second, Jesus endured an unjust death. Atonement for the sins of humanity required a trade of death for life. The sacrifice of innocent creatures was used in the Old Testament to wash away the imperfections of humanity in the eyes of God. Although the just wage for sin is death (Romans 6:23), God accepts a ransom as a means to pardon our sins. This ransom must include the shedding of blood (Hebrews 9:22).

Finally, God released Jesus from the grasp of death. The perfect sacrifice is not enough to merit eternal life. The resurrection was a critical step in the process of securing everlasting life. Bought with the death of the innocent, the pardon of sin was not cheap. The resurrection, however, made Jesus' sacrifice perpetual and our forgiveness everlasting.

Watchman Nee, a Chinese pastor, theologian, and author during the mid-1900s, points to Aaron's budding rod to illustrate resurrection as the basis of authority (Nee, 1971). The resurrection life of the budding rod signified Aaron's God-given authority, setting forth an architype of the resurrection life of Christ and His God-given authority to be the high priest of the redeemed. As Adam brought death to us all, the resurrection life of Jesus offers believers the hope of living again.

Victory Over Death

Death has its way with us all, and we are powerless to resist its call. The good news is death's call is not the final. Every person born of Adam must go the way of death, and those who are born again will follow Christ in resurrection (1 Corinthians 15:49). Salvation gives us victory over death and the grave. Although death remains an uncharted territory, that which is known overshadows the unknown. The believer, therefore, faces death with mixed emotions. We desire to stay in this world for those we love, yet we welcome death and the opportunity to live again (Philippians 1:23-24).

Life after death is far better than the life we live. The day approaches when we will be changed; our corruptible, mortal bodies will become incorruptible and immortal (1 Corinthians 15:53). The resurrection renders death impotent and destroys its power over the natural body. Corruption and decay will no longer be possible for the resurrected believer. This is the glorious victory given to us by God through the resurrection of His Son.

Therefore, death serves as a time of rest until believers are awakened by the triumphant return of the Risen Savior. He will return from heaven, and the dead in Christ – along with those who are living at the time – will ascend to meet Him in the air (1 Thessalonians 4:14-16). The curse of death will be lifted. Believers will celebrate victory over death and abide in the presence of the Lord forevermore.

New Jerusalem

Every Christian is destined for a unique path that leads to spiritual growth, but whatever the road, they all converge at a single destination, Heaven. Believers are bound together by their love for God as fellow citizens (Ephesians 2:19), and Heaven is their commonwealth. Heaven is home.

Moreover, Heaven is designed expressly for the family of God. Only there can one truly live life the way it was meant to be lived. God promises to wipe away all tears and do away with death, sorrow, crying, and pain. (Revelation 21:4). Heaven is the ultimate destination, even if we have to die to get there. It is to die for!

Heaven...Really?

Heaven is an amazing place; however, the term "heaven" can be deceiving. Are we using the term biblically? There are three surmisable heavens in scripture. Genesis 1:1 states that God created the heaven and the earth. Scriptural clues suggest that this heaven denotes outer space, often called the heaven of heavens.

Another heaven is seen in Genesis 1:8 where God separated ground water from atmospheric moisture. In order of elevation, birds fly "above the earth" in the first heaven; the sun, moon and stars occupy the second heaven (Genesis 1:14-18); and God sits on the throne in the third heaven (Revelation 4:2). The third heaven, as Paul calls it in 2 Corinthians 12:2, is the place where John received his revelation.

Peter tells us that the first and second heavens and the earth will be dissolved and replaced (2 Peter 3:12). Afterward, a holy Jerusalem will descend from God, from the new heaven onto the new earth (Revelation 21:10). It seems clear that Heaven, a place of eternal bliss, doesn't fit the description we have explored thus far. Could it be that when we say heaven, we really mean Paradise?

God gives a blessed promise in Revelation 2:7. Those who overcome trials and tribulations of this world will be given access to paradise – an ancient Persian word meaning "garden" (Strong's 3857) – and the fruit that adorns the tree of life. The heaven we envision is not suspended in the air, floating in space, nor in the throne room of God.

Heaven is paradise on a new earth. What was old will be new again.

The Old is New Again

The first paradise, the Garden of Eden, was a perfect place with perfect people, enjoying fellowship with a perfect God. The second paradise will be much the same: It will be occupied by perfect people, fellowshipping with a perfect God (Revelation 21:27). The first paradise featured the tree of life. The new paradise will restore the tree of life, bearing twelve types of fruit and leaves that can heal the nations (Revelation 22:2). The first paradise was without sin, death, and hell. The new paradise will be without sin, death, and hell (Revelation 20:14). Heaven is the product of the new Adam's labor to fix, through righteousness, what the first Adam broke with sin.

From Genesis to Revelation, God was and is working to restore what was lost in the Garden of Eden. The man God made corrupted His creation. Ever since that moment, God has guided humanity on a journey towards restoration. Whether we were willing participants or not, God was and is persistent.

As it was with Adam in the garden, so He destines it to be in Heaven. God will dispose of death, sorrow, crying, and pain (Revelation 21:3-4). Mankind will be restored. Our salvation – our journey from death to life – will finally be complete.

BIBLIOGRAPHY

Covey, Stephen A, et. al. 1994. *First Things First: To Live, to Love, to Learn, to Leave a Legacy.* New York: Simon and Schuster.

Easton, M. G. 1897. *Illustrated Bible Dictionary (also known as Easton's Bible Dictionary).* 3rd. London: T. Nelson & Sons.

Greenberg, Blu. 1981. *How to Run Traditional Jewish Households.* New York: Simon & Schuster.

Holton, James R. 1992. "An Introduction to Dynamic Meteorology." In *An Introduction to Dynamic Meteorology*, by James R. Holton, 11-12. Sandiego: ACADEMIC PRES.

Kee, Howard C. et al. 1998. *Christianity: A Social and Cultural History.* New Jersey: Prentice-Hall Inc.

Lang, Cedric. 2003. *The Time is Now: Doing the Best with What You Have.* Washington: Pleasant Wood.

Leach, Penelope. 2002. *Parents.* Accessed 5 28, 2018. www.parents.com.

Nee, Watchman. 1972. *Spiritual Authority.* New York: Christian Fellowship Publishers, Inc.

NIDA. 2003. *Preventing Drug Use among Children and Adolescents (In Brief)* . October 1. Accessed April 4, 2018. https://www.drugabuse.gov/publications/pre venting-drug-abuse-among-children-adolescents-in-brief/chapter-1-risk-factors-protective-factors/when-how-does-drug-abuse-start-progress.

Strong, James. 1800. *The Exhaustive Concordance of the Bible.* Cincinnati: Jennings & Graham.

U.S. Census Bureau. 2013. *Computer and internet Use in the United States: Population Characteristics.* May. Accessed April 4, 2018. https://www.census.gov/prod/2013pubs/p20-569.pdf.

9 781732 20040